THE CRAFT OF WINDOWS 95™ INTERFACE DESIGN

THE CRAFT OF WINDOWS 95™ INTERFACE DESIGN

Click Here to Begin

Alex Calvo

 Springer

Library of Congress Cataloging-in-Publication Data

Calvo, Alex
      The craft of Windows 95 interface design : click here to begin /
   Alex Calvo
         p.   cm
      Includes index.

      ISBN-13: 978-0-387-94814-0   e-ISBN-13: 978-1-4612-4060-0
      DOI: 10.1007/978-1-4612-4060-0

      1. Computer software–Development.   2. Microsoft Windows (Computer
   file)   I. Title
   QA76.76.D47C354   1996   96-19946
   005.2'65–dc20

Printed on acid-free paper.

Production managed by Steven Pisano; manufacturing supervised by Jeffrey Taub.
Photocomposed from the author's Microsoft Word files.

9 8 7 6 5 4 3 2 1

For Linda

> "Put your hands to work and your heart to God."
> – Shakers

Contents

◆ *Foreword* by Bart Barker xi

◆ *Introduction* xv

Chapter One
Shrink-Wrapped Design 1
  ◆ Then and Now 2
  📖 Click Here to Begin 6
    ❓ *Understanding the Problem* 6
    ❓ *Object-Oriented Design* 7
    ❓ *Following Standards* 8
    ❓ *Consistency* 9
    ❓ *Aesthetics* 10
    ❓ *The Devil Is in the Details* 14
    ❓ *Simplicity* 15
    ❓ *Finding the Right Words* 16
    ❓ *Learning from Others* 17
  ◆ Wrapping It Up 18

Chapter Two
The Interactive Canvas 19
  📖 Design Techniques 20
    ❓ *Side-By-Side Design* 20
    ❓ *Creating an Icon Museum* 21
    ❓ *Layout Comparison* 22
  📖 Tools of the Trade 24
    ❓ *Integrated Design Utilities* 24

? *Paint Programs*..26
? *The Windows Clipboard* 27
📖 Making an App an App...............................28
? *The Big Splash* 28
? *Toolbars* 30
? *UI Bulking* 31
? *Wrapping It Up*..32

Chapter Three
Following Guidelines..33
📖 Concise Windows 95 Interface Guidelines 35
? *Design Concepts*..35
? *Windows* 42
? *Controls*..52
? *Object Linking and Embedding*............................67
? *The Windows 95 Environment* 71
? *A Word About Windows NT* 84
? *The Windows 95 Logo Program* 85

Chapter Four
How to Help 91
📖 Designing Online Help...92
? *Context-Sensitive Help*..92
? *Help Topics*...99
? *Task Help*..104
? *Reference Help* 108
? *Wizards*..115
📖 Creating Online Help 120
? *Overview* 120
? *Rich-Text Format Files*..122
? *Microsoft Help Workshop*..126
? *Help Authoring Systems* 130
📖 Connecting Online Help...131

⁇ *Using the API* 131

⁇ *With Visual Basic* 132

Chapter Five

Prototyping 101 133

📖 Introduction to Microsoft Visual Basic 134

⁇ *Overview* 134

⁇ *Event-Driven Programming* 135

⁇ *Windows* 136

📖 Types of Prototypes...142

⁇ *Prototype? What Prototype?*...................................143

⁇ *Simple Screen Shots* 143

⁇ *Navigational Prototypes*..144

⁇ *Interactive Prototypes* 148

⁇ *Finding a Balance*..152

📖 Beyond Prototyping...152

⁇ *Developing with VB*...153

◆ *Epilogue*..155

◆ *Glossary* 159

◆ *Index* 179

Foreword

All you have is fifteen minutes.

In that time your software will succeed or fail. That's how long a consumer typically will spend with a hard to understand software program before setting it aside. And despite his intentions, once he has quit in confusion or frustration he is unlikely to try the product again. For the software publisher this means no word-of-mouth advertising, no upgrade sales, no more revenue from this consumer. The seriousness of this is clear to software publishers who understand that it is far easier and cheaper to retain a customer than to acquire a new one.

What constitutes good *graphical user interface* (GUI) design in software? That's what this book attempts to answer. Often it comes down to simply making user interface design a priority in the development process—understanding its importance and allocating sufficient time and resources to doing it right.

Designing the user interface correctly is important for both consumer software and in-house corporate software. Retail sales depend on consumer satisfaction. Corporate productivity requires efficient systems that engender accuracy and employee satisfaction. Although users often can't explain why they are more comfortable with one program than with another, usually it comes down to a sensible, consistent and thoughtful user interface design.

A few months ago I watched a product manager demonstrate a home banking product at a banking conference. He said: "The first thing you'll want to do is check your bank account balance. Just click here." He clicked the third button on the screen. If it was the first thing you would want to do, why was it the third button? Probably because *no one thought it through*. And once the system is designed, those close to it quickly adapt to its flaws and don't notice them. Of course you click the third button; it comes naturally to someone who has demonstrated the software 50 times. In a similar product from another company, the user sees six buttons with no indication what to do first or what to do next.

This sort of problem occurs frequently in software development. Designing the graphical interface seldom gets sufficient time and resources in a software project. The design may be rushed, or performed by someone without expertise, or done as an afterthought by a programmer who is unaware of market or customer needs.

It still is not unusual for each programmer to create a unique interface for her section of the program. A scrolling list in one part of the software jumps to the first matching entry when you type a letter on the keyboard. On other lists typing in a list doesn't do anything. And this is a minor inconsistency. Even when customers don't notice an inconsistency, it can subtly affect productivity, accuracy, comfort with the program, or enjoyment while using it—or all four.

Most companies that produce software for the retail consumer market at least attempt to design good graphical interfaces. It happens less often in a corporate environment, where the data processing department develops applications for use only within the company. These customer databases, order-entry programs, manufacturing control systems, and other in-house programs don't have to compete in an open marketplace. The "customers" are employees who must use the software to do their jobs and who can't choose an alternative product. The MIS staff may not even have an interface design expert.

Although poorly designed software often results, employees may not complain because it always has been this way. The software is always hard to learn and awkward to use, so employees receive training. But awkward computer-human interaction surely causes an unthinkable loss in worker productivity, many data entry and processing errors, and unnecessarily high training and support costs. The study and application of "human factors"—the way people interact with computers and machines—ought to be a top priority for those developing in-house automation.

Several years ago, when MECA Software was developing its first Windows version of *Managing Your Money* (a personal finance program), the company had no one whose job was to design the user interface. Alex Calvo, a programmer with a Macintosh background, stepped into that role. He was responsible for designing the interface to most of Version 1. His talent was so obvious that when he left the company for entrepreneurial pursuits, the company created a design department to institutionalize the standards Alex set. The result was a product that won awards for its easy, clean, and consistent interface.

Alex Calvo employed the same design talent in designing the software developed by his own company, fyi Software. Now, in this book, he shares his insight.

Bart Barker

Bart Barker is responsible for the development of Home ATM, Home Pay, *and other home banking products known for their wonderfully simple graphical interfaces. He allocated three months of design for every month of programming these products. He is vice president and general manager of research and de-*

velopment at Home Financial Network, based in Westport, Conn. Previously he organized and led the design department at MECA Software, publisher of Managing Your Money. *He assumed MECA's design duties after working several years with Andrew Tobias, the original creator of* Managing Your Money.

Introduction

The journey to becoming a better interface designer is one of self-discovery.
We all have a natural sense of beauty
deep inside our hearts. Uncovering it,
however, requires much effort and desire
on your part. I hope that, in reading this
book, you discover that you've become
a better designer.

Welcome to *The Craft of Windows 95 Interface Design*!

This book's primary intent is to present you with a practical (and
sometimes philosophical) approach to interface design. Although
the book focuses on Windows 95 software, some of the information takes on a more generic point of view. After all, you can't
change the fact that good design is simply that, regardless of what
you're designing. Whether it's a Windows 95 application or a brochure for a new product, many of the same design principles can be
applied in both situations.

The main reason I wrote this book is to help combat the increase of
ugly software. Bad design can make us feel bad, sometimes consciously and oftentimes subconsciously. And, unfortunately, as the
number of PCs running Windows continues its incessant rise, so
does the amount of poorly designed software that is being developed for them.

The advent of visual development tools have allowed a plethora of inexperienced programmers and new software companies to create some pretty homely looking products. This is not to say, however, that a more experienced programmer or a larger software firm does not suffer from the same maladies—quite the contrary. I can think of quite a few well known Windows applications developed by competent people at the biggest software houses that make me yearn for the days of DOS.

In the end, you'll find that the answer to good software design exists somewhere between the left brain and the right brain. This balance is the key to designing applications that are both intuitive and aesthetically appealing. Without both of these things, the success of a program—whether it's measured in number of units sold or the enthusiasm of a user—will be more and more dependent on how much money there is to back it up and less and less reliant on how good the product really is. How is it that one person, or worse yet, a group of individuals, some of whom are more technical and others are more artistic, can ever find this balancing point? This book will help you do just that.

Although the need for an easy to use interface is quite clear, the need for an aesthetically appealing interface may not be as evident. Whether you're a programmer, a project leader, a product manager, a consultant, a graphic designer, or a budding entrepreneur (did I miss anyone there?) this book will try to maximize your interface design capabilities. Before you begin on your journey, let's take a quick look at each chapter. Good luck!

Introduction

(You are here.)

Chapter One—Shrink-Wrapped Design

It'll probably come as no surprise that this was the first chapter I wrote, because it is, after all, Chapter One. Chapter One is all about attitude readjustment. How you look at things is how others will see them. I want this chapter to quickly grab you by introducing you to the importance of interface design and how it has evolved over the last decade. Then, immediately after that, I show you things that you can do to really make a difference in your design. By the time you finish this chapter, you'll have become familiar not only with the reasons why interface design is so important, but also some of the things you can do to design a better interface.

Most of the design concepts presented in this chapter are of a general nature and do not apply exclusively to Windows 95.

Chapter Two—The Interactive Canvas

In Chapter Two, you'll be introduced to the tools and techniques that go into designing an interface for a Windows 95 application. By the time you finish Chapter Two, you'll have a better understanding of the design process as a whole and what's involved in creating an application that comes across as a savvy product rather than just another ordinary program.

The interactive canvas is the place where you turn your software ideas into reality. Many of the ideas I discuss in this chapter aren't things you can find in any other book. They are techniques I've developed over the years, while designing my own software.

Chapter Three—Following Guidelines

When it comes to designing software for Windows 95, this chapter is the meat and potatoes of the book. Here you'll find a concise look at the Windows 95 interface guidelines and how they can be used to design a product worthy of wearing the "Designed for Microsoft Windows 95" logo.

Instead of presenting ideas and concepts using a big reference manual, which most of us will never actually read from cover to cover, my approach tries to be much more lighthearted and easily digestible (I hope). That'll be one order of menu buttons and a side order of progress bars to go, please.

Chapter Four—How To Help

To me, interface design runs the gamut of all the visible aspects of an application. Because of this, I've included a chapter dedicated entirely to designing an effective online help system for your Windows 95 compatible software.

In some respects, the changes that took place in the Windows 95 help system were even more drastic than the changes that took place in other areas of the Windows 95 interface. For this reason, I've tried to present the new help system in a way that will clarify the differences between it and the old Windows 3.1 help system.

The chapter finishes up by unraveling the mysteries of how you actually create a help system in Windows 95.

Chapter Five—Prototyping 101

As I looked around at other interface design books, it seemed that most of them were skipping over an important aspect of the design process: prototyping. This chapter teaches you what you need to know and how you go about creating an effective prototype using a tool such as Microsoft Visual Basic.

After being introduced to the most popular prototyping tool in history, we'll discuss the different levels of interactivity and how they can have an impact on the presentation of your design ideas.

Epilogue

I refuse to give any more of the book away. You'll have to read it if you really want to know what it's about...

And that's pretty much it—the book in a nutshell—if you will. As you can see, its structure is rather simple and it's meant to be the kind of book that you can read from cover to cover. Sure, there will be a few sections that are too technical for casual reading by the fireplace. But the good thing is that they're short and they're packed with a lot of information. Enjoy the book!

CHAPTER ONE

Shrink-Wrapped Design

Given two competitive software products, one that is ugly and hard to use and another that has a well-designed interface, most users will opt for the better design regardless of slight variations in number of features and/or performance.

Why "Shrink-Wrapped Design" you might ask? The answer is quite simple: because, nowhere else in the world of design is the look and feel of a product more important than it is in the land of retail software. The fierce competition that exists in this market has given us some of the best human engineering concepts known to man. Even if your software is not consumer-oriented, you should still put this kind of effort into its design. By doing so, you'll be sure to make your users happy and, at the same time, help pave your way to success. In the end, you'll need to ask yourself just one question, "Is this program good enough to be a Microsoft product?" Because, like it or not, Microsoft is the standard by which all other software products are judged.

You would think that by now most software companies would understand the importance of good interface design or, better yet, what constitutes good design. Unfortunately, this is not the case. This chapter introduces you to a variety of basic design concepts that can help transform a program into a savvy software product. But first, let's take a look at the history of interface design and some of the reasons why it has become such a problematic area.

Then and Now

Back in the old days, character-based systems, such as DOS, automatically provided a certain amount of conformity and consistency between applications. You would seldom come across an application that was very different from the rest. The limited display capabilities did not allow for much artistic freedom on the part of the software designer. With only 25 rows by 80 columns of characters there wasn't much room to get creative with an interface—at least this made it easy to line things up. Also, the plethora of font choices we have today was nonexistent then, and the number of colors available was limited at best.

Then, almost overnight, IBM-compatible software began to take on a new look by utilizing the extended ASCII character set. New, character-based interface objects became commonplace. Developers now had to deal with other decisions in addition to what algorithm or memory management scheme to use. With a slew of different character-based interface objects to choose from, such as buttons and movable windows, screen design quickly became an integral part of the software design process. Unfortunately, most of these new character-based interfaces were all home-grown. With each and every program looking and behaving differently from the rest, widespread inconsistency made learning a new program a difficult task to master.

With the advent of the graphical user interface, particularly Windows 3.0, the number of choices that could be made by a developer went through the roof. Colors, icons, bitmaps, fonts, and hundreds of controls now provide the developer with a virtual canvas on which to paint an application's interface. Did you know that on the average screen there are over 300,000 (640 x 480 pixels) different locations in which an object can be placed? Talk about lining things up! It's no wonder why it's easy to overlook a pixel here and a pixel there.

We are now at a point in time when the look and feel of a software product can make or break its success. With all other things being equal, a product that has a poorly designed interface will have a hard time succeeding against a well-designed counterpart. Think of automobiles; it's usually the ugly ones that don't sell very well, oftentimes regardless of how well they're built—that is, if you're not counting Swedish cars, which manage to sell well despite their boxy appearance.

In addition, the look and feel of a software product can literally define the designer. Each product is like a work of art, on display for the whole world to see. Your signature is written all over it, in the way you use controls, the colors you choose for icons, how carefully you line things up, the wording of your text, and, not to forget, how consistent you are. These are the choices you make and the things by which your work is judged.

The evolution of interface design as seen in three of the most popular personal finance products...

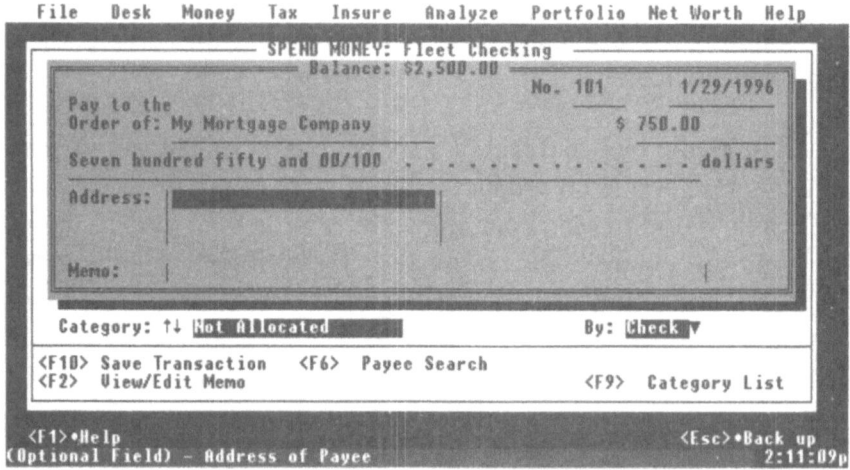

MECA Software's Managing Your Money 10 for DOS is a prime example of a character-based (pseudographical) interface.

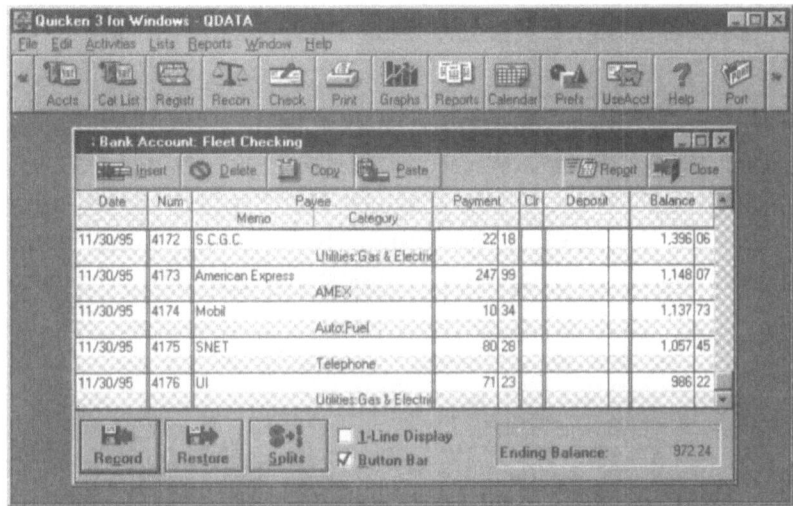

Quicken 3.0 for Windows by Intuit. Icon-based design, such as this, still remains extremely popular with users and developers.

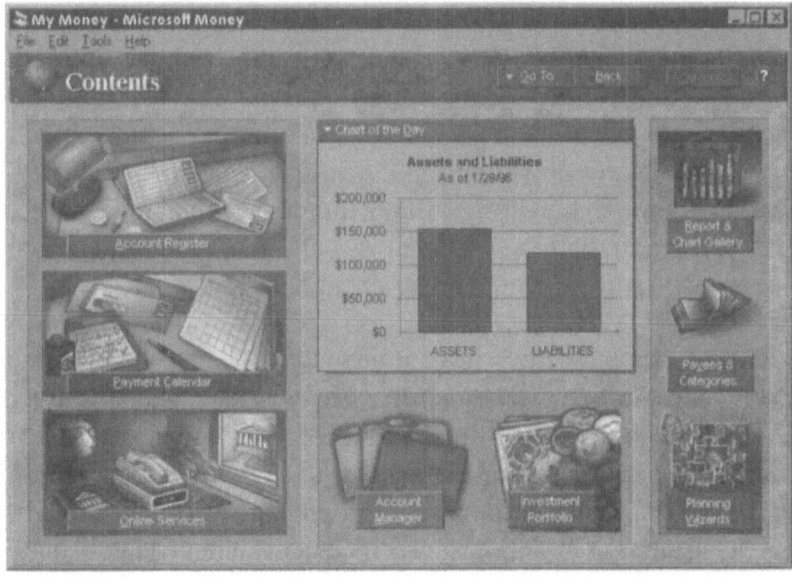

Microsoft Money 95 sports a savvy multimedia-like interface.

Click Here To Begin

What better way to get started than to jump right in? In this section, we take a close look at a variety of design concepts that you can begin using right away. Unlike Chapter Three, where we examine the Windows 95 interface guidelines, these concepts are much more generic and can be applied to almost any graphical user interface.

Understanding the Problem

An application must first and foremost get its job done. To accomplish this, the developer must thoroughly understand the problem for which the program is to provide a solution. Without that, nothing that this book has to offer is of any use.

Thoroughly understanding the problem will involve much research and brainstorming. It is essential that everyone involved in the product's development is on the same wavelength in order to avoid costly product delays down the road. Minor misunderstandings today could become major design flaws tomorrow. Imagine a medical billing system that was designed with the assumption that Medicare and Medicaid would never change!

The software designer must have a clear mental map of both the forest and the trees. A designer can get caught up with the little details and ignore the overall picture—I know. I've been guilty of this. Sometimes you can care more about a single icon than you do about the entire product. Likewise, a product may be well thought out but have no real attention given to its aesthetics. This usually happens when the company attitude is, "Don't waste your time worrying about that junk," or, "That's not real work." The fact is that interface design is very real work, and the benefits that good design can provide make it well worth worrying about.

| Object-Oriented Design |

Once you thoroughly understand the problem the software is to address, the interface design process should begin by dividing the things that go into solving that problem into two logical groups: objects (nouns) and tasks (verbs). Objects are the things that the program lets you work with: a database of customers, a column of numbers, a hard disk. Tasks are the things that the program lets you do to those objects: look up a customer, add some numbers, defragment a hard drive. Searching for the optimal way to visually present these two items is the key to good interface design.

Begin by making a list of every word that pops into your head with respect to the program you are designing. Sort your list into these two groups (objects and tasks) as best you can. Then look for the relationships and similarities between objects and how they fit together. If you find lots of overlap between objects, try combining them into one. For example, imagine that you are designing an application for a law firm. Two of the objects in your list are Clients and Friends. Because clients may also be friends and vice versa, consider combining these two objects into one object called Address Book, especially if they share many of the same database fields. Each entry in Address Book could then have a check box indicating whether they are a friend. This would provide the user with a simpler paradigm and at the same time allow for a cleaner interface.

If, on the other hand, you have listed too many compound objects (objects comprised of smaller objects), consider breaking them down into their various components. For example, imagine that one of your interface objects, Contracts, is too general. Depending on the particular law firm, it may be more effective to split this into two parts, Government Contracts and Business Contracts, especially if they have nothing to do with each other and have few similarities.

As your list of objects becomes more and more refined, so should your list of tasks that are associated with each object. For example, our Address Book object should be able to perform the following tasks: Add, Delete, Find, Print, and so on. These tasks can later be transformed into buttons and menu items, providing the user with a means to execute his or her commands.

By understanding the problem and being able to map it out into these two groups, half the battle is already won. Looking at the problem in this manner will definitely improve your design capabilities and allow you to see things more clearly. Because people naturally tend to think of objects using a noun/verb relationship, attempting to model your interface in a more *data-centric* fashion will help you lay the groundwork for an easy to use application.

Following Standards

Nothing attracts attention more than something that is out of place: a bright red Ferrari parked outside a shack or a gardener wearing a tuxedo. Although sometimes it's good to be different and become a trendsetter, you are putting yourself in a position to be scrutinized and may end up paying a price. With each nonstandard choice you make, you risk offending a user who has come to expect a certain behavior from his or her applications.

You might think using a stop sign instead of a cancel button is a neat idea, but it's typically these kinds of offenses that make a user hate a certain program and at the same time, ironically, love another. Unfortunately, it's sometimes hard to make a judgment call about which route to take. In this case, are there more people like you, who love stop signs, or more who hate them?

The lesson to be learned is this: be very careful, and make sure that if you are doing something different and nonstandard that it is by choice and not by ignorance.

(For a quick look at the Microsoft Windows interface guidelines, the standards by which your program will be judged, see Chapter Three.)

Consistency

Inconsistency is another offense that can really crawl under a user's skin. Although this is a more subtle offense, it is no less bothersome than a blatant disregard of the standards. In fact, being consistently inconsistent can not only drive your users crazy, it can make your program needlessly difficult to use. Picture a program with a "Find Customer" button along the bottom of the window. In another window, the button appears along the top and reads "Customer Look up." Each time your users encounter something different, more of their time has to be spent thinking about how to use the program instead of why they are using it in the first place.

As you design your interface keep a mental list or, better yet, a written list of all the things you do, always thinking ahead and asking yourself, "Will I be doing this again later on?" Consistency in things like capitalization, button placement, colors used to draw attention, and font attributes (bold, italics, underlines), is very easy to overlook, especially a few weeks down the road.

I think you get the point; consistency will give the user a feeling of security. The more consistent an application is, the quicker the user will be able to learn it and become more productive.

Aesthetics

Icons are the heart of a graphical user interface. They facilitate the user's ability to quickly and efficiently navigate a program while providing a high level of intuitiveness. Icons also provide a mechanism of personality for the program. Long after we've left our computers, these tiny little mosaic images are often what we think of when we picture an application. More than anything else, icons are what makes an application attractive or ugly.

When designing a new icon, the best rule of thumb is to keep it simple. I'm sure you've heard the saying, "Don't bite off more than you can chew." Instead of trying to draw a teacher in front of a blackboard, perhaps a simple question mark would be more appropriate for a help icon, not to mention a lot easier to implement.

Nothing will improve your icon design techniques more than practice, practice, and more practice. As time goes on, you will be able to create just about anything your imagination desires. Designing these tiny 32 x 32 pixel mosaics using only 16 base colors takes a lot of time and patience. Here are a couple of icon design techniques you can start using right away:

Anti-aliasing...

When trying to draw a curve or a diagonal line in such a small space, the pixels can often create a jagged and rough appearance. You can combat these so-called *jaggies* by using a technique known as anti-aliasing. Notice, in the picture above, how the black jagged pixels have been replaced with shades of gray in order to smooth into the white background. This creates the illusion of a less jagged line by tricking your eye with a fine blur. As a rule of thumb, you can anti-alias most jaggies by using colors that best match the average color of the adjoining pixels.

Keep in mind, however, that there are only 16 base icon colors in Windows (black, white, and dual shades of gray, red, green, blue, cyan, magenta, and yellow) and finding an average color is often impossible. For this reason, it is a good idea to use a black outline around whatever it is you are drawing, especially if it has lots of jaggies. Then, by using the darker shade of the adjoining color, you can anti-alias the black jaggies.

You can use this table to help combat the jaggies in your icons...

Pixel color	If the adjoining pixel is darker, try using:	If the adjoining pixel is brighter, try using:
Black	n/a	Either Gray
White	Either Gray	n/a
Gray	Dark Gray	n/a
Dark Gray	n/a	Gray
Red	Dark Red	Magenta
Dark Red	Dark Gray	Red
Green	Dark Green	Light Gray
Dark Green	Dark Gray	Green
Blue	Dark Blue	Light Gray
Dark Blue	Dark Gray	Blue
Cyan	Dark Cyan	Light Gray
Dark Cyan	Dark Gray	Cyan
Yellow	Dark Yellow	Light Gray
Dark Yellow	Dark Gray	Yellow
Magenta	Dark Magenta	Light Gray
Dark Magenta	Dark Gray	Magenta

Dithering...

Combining different colored pixels in a small area allows you to simulate new and unique shades of colors. This technique is known as dithering. You can greatly improve the look and feel of your icons by dithering the 16 base colors. This technique makes it appear as though you used many more colors. Notice how, in the picture above, by simply using black and white pixels we can create a shade of gray. Believe it or not, the two boxes appear to be the same color when held at a distance.

Blends...

Dithering can also help you create blends between two colors. The black and white pixels in the picture above are diffused as they come together. The transition progresses from 100% black pixels, to 75% black (25% white), 50% black (50% white), 25% black (75% white), and finally 100% white pixels. This is a great way to create a background horizon for your icon designs. Try using yellow and white, or cyan and white, and you'll see just how dramatic this can be.

Lighting...

All three-dimensional interface objects should adhere to one common trait: the light source. The above picture demonstrates the Windows common light source, which shines from the top left of the screen to the bottom right-most corner. Notice how shadows can be added to give the feeling of depth. When all objects are shaded according to the same light source, a subtle sense of realism and balance is perceived by the user. Taking advantage of this light source in your icon designs can really add polish to your application's interface.

There are numerous ways in which you could incorporate this light source into your icon designs. When adding a three-dimensional object to your icon, be sure that it is shaded appropriately. To do this, use a light shade for the top of the object, a medium shade for its front, and a dark shade for its right or lower side. Likewise, two-dimensional objects should also respect the common light source. Adding a drop-shadow using dark gray along the lower right outer edge of an object is a great and easy way to add depth to a two-dimensional object.

Real-World Issue:
How do you attach an icon to a window?

This depends on the development system you're using. For example, in Microsoft Visual Basic you simply set the Icon property of a form.

The Devil Is in the Details

I was recently looking at a new car brochure and couldn't help but notice all the talk about the millimeter tolerance levels between adjoining body panels. How well things fit together has always been a characteristic of quality in the consumer's eyes, and the car company knew enough to stress that point for potential customers. Nothing could be more analogous to the placement of your controls on a dialog or window. As they say, "The devil is in the details." It's very often these tiny little details that get left out as one rushes to deliver an application on time. How many times have you seen it? Text boxes that aren't all the same height. A button that's a pixel or two smaller than the rest. Check boxes that don't line up with one another. It's very easy to overlook such minute differences when trying to meet a deadline. Unfortunately, your users will notice, either consciously or subconsciously.

Simplicity

Simplicity is at the core of good interface design. Too many bells and whistles can make the user feel as though more time was spent on fun and games rather than on a solution to the problem. As we said before, your time is much better spent concentrating on the problem at hand than it is on too many details.

Adding unnecessary flash to a product may seem like a good idea at first, but try using it day after day. Chances are that what once seemed pretty neat will eventually become a nuisance and will begin to get on your nerves. In the end, you want your users to see your product as the sum of its parts, not as individual instances of gaudiness.

Because not everybody has the same sense of beauty, keeping things simple also allows your interface to be accepted by more users. Take furniture as an example. If you decorate your home using a Victorian theme, even though you love it, chances are that with all of its intricate details, some of your visitors will be sure to hate it. On the other hand, if you use a simpler design theme, such as with Shaker furniture, your home will likely be admired by more people. Instead of having each detail stand out so loudly, a simple decorating theme allows the room's overall design to make an impression. Keeping your interface as simple as possible will, in the same way, offend less and be praised by more.

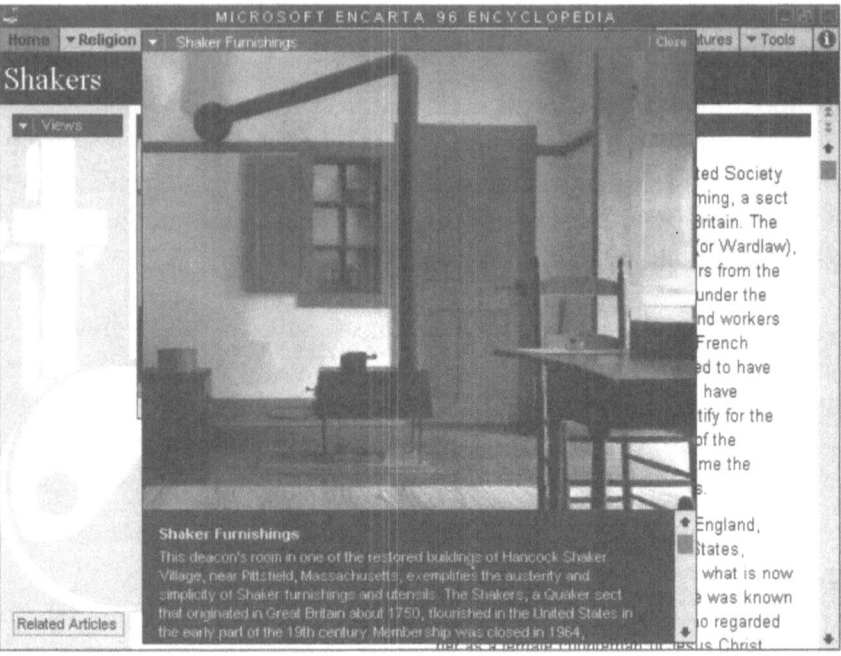

The remarkable simplicity of Shaker furniture design, as seen in Microsoft Encarta 96, can be applied to interface design.

Finding the Right Words

The words you choose for your interface are of vital essence. Ultimately, these are the biggest cue a user has when learning to use a new program. From button names to group box captions, text must be carefully and thoughtfully chosen. Be careful not to be overly verbose, for this is sure to clutter the screen and frustrate the more experienced user. Simplicity is best when choosing words. Be consistent and employ the object-oriented methodology mentioned earlier. For example, when the user clicks on a button, he or she is doing something, hence the button's caption should be task-oriented—"Find Customer" (or just plain "Find")—instead of object-oriented—"Customer" (even "Customer Search" puts too much emphasis on the noun). Again, keep the number of words to a minimum; there is no need to say "Find a Customer."

Learning from Others

Notice how I didn't say "copying from others." There's a big difference between the two. Obviously, ripping off someone else's interface can be an outright infringement of the copyright laws. In addition, you don't want to end up in a situation where you're always chasing your competition's tail. Instead, let them chase yours for a change. Nevertheless, learning from other great software products is an excellent way to become a better designer. You should always keep up with the latest technology and trends. You can do this by studying today's most popular software titles. Take notes about what you like and dislike about them or how they handle a particular interface situation. Studying great products is the way to stay ahead of your competition.

By mixing and matching the most successful interface trends, your product will be sure to have a cutting-edge look. Think of the tool bar as an example; its widespread popularity has allowed many applications to become easier to use and, at the same time, more attractive. It's hard to believe the tool bar was once one person's idea and was used in only one product! Do you remember what product that was? Incorporating great interface ideas (which have already proven themselves) into your own software is a good way to ensure the acceptance of your design.

As new ideas become popular, evolution takes place, with bad ideas being left behind and good ones prevailing. Like an invisible hand, this selective process is constantly guiding interface design in the direction of intuitiveness and aesthetics.

Wrapping It Up

Obviously, not every program ends up on a shelf at CompUSA or Egghead Software. Maybe you're developing an internal client/server product, or perhaps a vertical market application for the medical industry; the list goes on and on. However, regardless of who your target audience is, you should always design your software as though it were going to be on a shelf alongside some pretty stiff competition. This will force you to make sure that your software is both attractive and user-friendly. As long as you're creating a program that will be used by people other than yourself, you should design it as though it were going to be used by a million users.

Successful software companies have learned the value of good interface design. Loads of money has been spent on focus groups, usability tests, and surveys. Companies have created entire divisions dedicated solely to human interface engineering. They've come to realize that the interface is the embodiment of the product.

By paying attention to the points made in this chapter, you will be rewarded in many ways and well on your way to creating a great software product. Peers will admire you, your boss will value your sense of design, and, most of all, you'll be able to take pride in your work.

CHAPTER TWO

The Interactive Canvas

With new and exciting video technology always on the horizon, user interface design is continually evolving. This makes the art of interface design even more challenging and difficult to master.

Think of interface design as an interactive canvas. In the past this canvas would often burden the software designer, but now its capabilities are becoming virtually boundless. With the advent of so many new *visual* programming environments, such as Microsoft Visual Basic and Borland's Delphi, the modern day software designer can literally *paint* an application's interface on the screen. Long gone are the days of manually entering the position and size of objects and then having to wait for the computer to compile your program, only to find out that things didn't come out quite as you had planned.

Whereas the previous chapter focused on basic interface design concepts, this chapter deals with design techniques on a more pragmatic level. How can you enforce a consistent look and feel across all products? What's the most efficient way to determine the best screen layout? What tools are needed to create a great interface? How can you make an application look as if it has more functionality and at the same time be easier to use? The solutions to these real-world design problems will help you develop a solid technique, and enable you to bring an application's interface to life in the shortest possible amount of time.

Design Techniques

The following design tips are techniques that I've developed over the last few years to help make my software look like it was developed by a software giant. These tips will help give your interface the high quality look and feel that is typically found in many successful software titles.

Side-by-Side Design

As you start to design your application, you will begin to accumulate many different screen layouts, icons, and bitmaps. In the process of doing so, you may find yourself deviating from your original style or from the style used by your other products. This can happen because of forgetfulness, boredom, lor just ignorance.

To prevent this from happening, use a side-by-side design technique. With each new visual entity you create, go back and take a look at everything else that you've created to that point (previous products, screen layouts, icons, etc.). Analyze the details for things such as button placement, vocabulary, capitalization, and colors. If you're creating a new screen, make sure that you view it in context and not just by itself. For example, where will it appear? In front of a particular window, perhaps? Using side-by-side design will constantly remind you of your previous design efforts. When everything fits together well, your software is seen as a holistic product and not just as if it had been slapped together by 50 different people, all with a different design in mind. The side-by-side design technique is a great way to make your users feel as though you have a great, quality-oriented software company.

Using the side-by-side design technique to enforce a consistent look and feel really does not take that much extra effort. Initially it may seem a bit tedious to constantly go back and refer to your previous work but, eventually, it will become second nature and you'll hardly notice any delays in productivity. And, over time, your style will become embedded in your mind.

Creating an Icon Museum

The look and feel of your icons and bitmaps can make your application appear either polished and consistent or shoddy and visually unstable. Creating an icon museum is a great way to make sure your application ends up looking professional. By using a paint program to maintain a file containing all of your application's icons and bitmaps, you have, in effect, created an icon museum!

Traditionally, a separate icon editor is used for creating icons. An icon editor is a lot like a paint program with the exception that you have a lot less elbow room in which to work. This is because most icons are only 32 x 32 or 16 x 16 pixels in size. The main reason why you can't use a paint program to directly open and save icon files is because an icon file (.ico) can include a variety of image sizes. In addition, icon editors provide two extra colors that are typically not available from a paint program: a transparent color and an inverted color. The transparent color allows you to designate an area in the icon that will let the background show through. In other words, an image behind an icon can be seen through the transparent color. The inverted color, on the other hand, will invert the background image.

Instead of creating each and every icon separately with an icon editor, consider using your paint program as a canvas for all your

icon designs. Chances are that one full screen in your paint program will be plenty big enough to store just about every icon and
bitmap in your application. In one glimpse, you will be able to ensure that all your graphics have a consistent look and feel.

Not only will you be employing side-by-side design by having all
your icons next to each other, but you will also be able to conven-
iently leverage off your previous graphics because they are all right
there in the same file. By using the clipboard, you will be able to
easily copy different parts of your old icons and create new and
unique ones in a snap!

Seeing all your previous icons together is a great way to keep the look
and feel of your graphics consistent with each other.

Layout Comparison

Design can only be perfected through constant repetition and
analysis. Looking at a screen in as many different ways as possible
is the best way to truly be sure that you have chosen its optimal

layout. For example, do these buttons look best along the right side of the window or along the bottom? Does this graphic look best over here or over there? The only real way to answer these types of questions is by actually seeing the difference. Only then will you be sure you have found the perfect balance.

In this way, the interface designer is a lot like an architect; he must decide where to place the many windows and doors within the larger context of the floor plan. Rarely would you find an architect who does not consider more than one layout option. Stopping at the first version of a screen layout is like sketching a floor plan and never rearranging any of it.

You can play around with your screen layouts using either your development system's integrated design utility or with a paint program. I prefer to use a paint program for layout comparisons. What I usually do is create the basic layout of controls using the development environment, copy the screen to the clipboard (using **Alt+PrintScrn**), and then paste it into my paint program. It is much more efficient to run multiple instances of the paint program than it is the development system. This makes it easier to compare many different variations of the same screen. Once I've found the one that works best, I go back to the development system and finalize the design.

Tools of the Trade

Whether you're a designer, project leader, product manager, or a real live programmer, one thing should be quite evident: you must have a clear understanding of your development system's interface design capabilities. How else can you know if the interface you're envisioning for your application is even remotely possible? It's easy when you're naive to say something like, "Let's go ahead and make plastic purple widgets," not knowing, all the while, that the widget machine only supports untinted alloys.

Many times people have asked for the world in seven days only to be waiting for it seven months down the road. Take the plastic purple widgets as an example. Sure, you can have them if you really want. Just don't be expecting them anytime soon. You must be realistic about your software design if it is ever going to reach your user's desktop.

To design a great interface you'll need to master three basic tools: your development system's design utility, a halfway decent paint program, and the Windows clipboard.

Integrated Design Utilities

The first tool you'll need to conquer is your development system's integrated design utility. With the advent of the visual programming language, almost every popular development environment (e.g., Microsoft Visual Basic, Visual C++, Visual FoxPro, and Borland Delphi), provides some type of way to interactively place controls on a blank window. Although tools like Visual Basic and Delphi have built-in control palettes, others, like Visual C++, include a separate resource editor for laying out screens. Nevertheless, these screen design utilities all work in a similar manner. The user simply selects controls from a palette of available choices and places them on a new blank window. The types of controls you can use is largely dependent on the development system you're using. However, most, if not all, of them will include a basic set of controls, such as command buttons, edit boxes, and list boxes.

Although they may differ in some ways, most development systems also support what are known as *custom controls*. Custom controls allow you to add new and exciting controls that can help set your application apart from the rest. There are two basic types of custom controls available: Visual Basic custom controls (VBX), which are slightly older, and OLE custom controls (OCX).

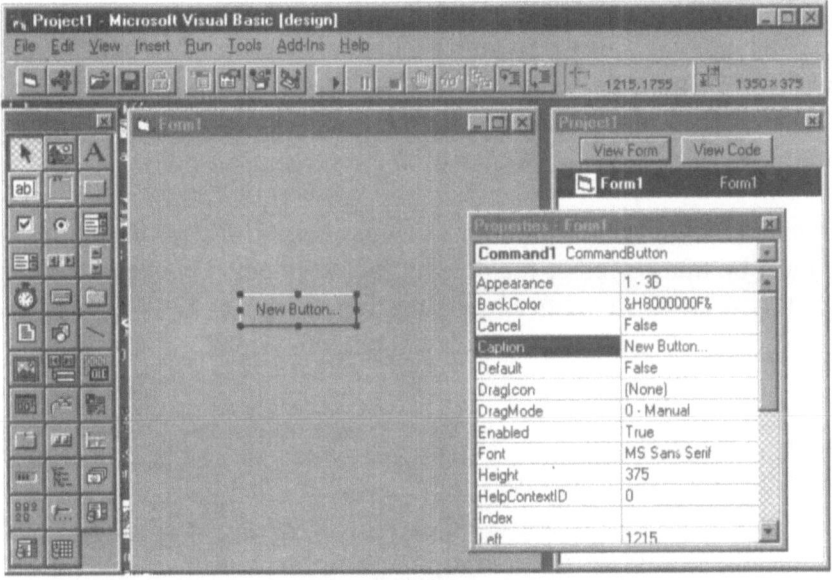

Microsoft's Visual Basic was one of the first development environments to incorporate a tightly integrated interface design mode.

(For a close look at Microsoft Visual Basic see Chapter Five—Prototyping 101.)

Paint Programs

The other tool that you'll need is a good paint program that allows you to create and manipulate both 16-color and 256-color bitmaps. You will often need to modify an image one pixel at a time, so make sure that the paint program you choose allows for this kind of low-level manipulation. (I like to use the Paint utility that comes with Windows 95.) A paint program is a vital element of the interface design process. It is the foundry of all graphical elements in your program, from icons to bitmaps.

A paint program also provides a quick way to create *what-if* scenarios. What if this were red instead of blue? What if this were here instead of there? Sometimes the only way to decide on something like that is to actually see it on the screen.

Once an image has been created or modified with a paint program, it must be transferred to the development system. This can be done via the Windows clipboard (see the following) or by opening the graphics file directly from the development system.

Real-World Issue:
Designing in 256 colors...

When creating 256-color bitmaps, make sure that they all use the same palette (preferably the Windows system palette). This keeps an application from flashing palettes when running in 256-color mode.

The Windows Clipboard

Although it's not a separate program or utility, the Windows clipboard is also an important aspect of the interface design process. Everybody has at one time or another used the clipboard to copy and paste text within a word processor or between different applications. The clipboard also allows you to transfer graphics from the paint program to the development system. By using the **Alt+PrintScrn** keyboard command, you can even copy an image of the current active window to the clipboard and then paste it into your paint program. Why would you want to do this? Because using the clipboard to capture a snapshot of the screen provides an easy and effective way to try different things from within your paint program.

Take the word processor I am using now as an example. By pressing the **Alt+PrintScrn** keys simultaneously, I can capture an image of the screen and then paste it into the Paintbrush accessory. This would allow me to quickly rearrange the toolbar, change colors, or add a hypothetical feature. All this without ever touching the development environment. (Of course, I couldn't do that anyway, because I don't have the code to Microsoft Word.)

Making an App an App

What is it that makes one program look like a school project and another look so professional? (Not to imply that school projects can't be professional.) Certainly it has to be more than just what we've talked about. In this section take a quick look at the shortest way to get from point A to point B. By simply doing the things discussed in this section, you can turn what would otherwise be a faceless program into a more marketable application—assuming you have a halfway decent idea.

The Big Splash

Just about every great software product starts with some kind of splash screen. The splash screen is to software what a cover is to a book. And although "you can't judge a book by its cover," everybody usually does. A splash screen allows a program to introduce itself to a user during startup. Think of it as the application's name tag saying something friendly such as, "Hi, I'm your favorite program!"

By having a splash screen display as soon as the user double-clicks on the application icon, your program can appear faster than it would otherwise, because a splash screen distracts the user while the application loads into memory. This is a perfect example of the duality of form and function. Not only can the splash screen add pizzazz and beauty to your application, but it also deals with the real world issue of startup time.

Choosing the right graphic for your splash screen is a critical mission. The moment the user sees the splash screen she begins to anticipate what's in store for her. Remember to keep it simple, the user will see the splash screen every time she runs the application. As was said earlier, what once seemed pretty neat will eventually become a nuisance and really begin to get on a user's nerves.

If your splash screen image uses 256 colors or more, try to include a 16-color rendition for the good old VGA guys. Or, dither the 256-color image down to the standard 16-color VGA palette—this is quite popular these days. Splash screens that have a similar look to the retail packaging tend to work rather well. Finally, no matter how good you are at designing interfaces, don't be afraid to have someone else design the splash screen; it's really an art unto itself.

The Microsoft Windows 3.1 splash screen is perhaps the most famous splash screen of all time.

Real-World Issue:
Saving resources...

Consider using the same window (or graphic) for both the splash screen and the about box. This eliminates the need to maintain two windows.

Toolbars

Adding a toolbar is an easy way to put the user in control of your application (the way it should be), not the other way around. Everybody has seen a toolbar at this point and, even though they are hardly a new thing, they are still extremely popular and a favorite among many users.

A toolbar allows your users to navigate quickly and easily throughout your program. Toolbars have come to be what is considered a de facto standard in modern day interface design. Long gone are the days of only providing pull-down menus. So if your product doesn't have a toolbar, it darn well better have something else in its place.

Be sure that your toolbar provides instant feedback to the user with regard to what action each button performs. There are quite a few ways you can do this.

If your toolbar's buttons have no text, you can use tool tips as Microsoft does.

In addition, you can use a status bar at the bottom of the window.

Or, you can display text on your toolbar buttons, the way MECA Software's Managing Your Money for Windows does.

UI Bulking

These days users have come to expect a lot from their software, especially when they are paying for it themselves. "UI Bulking" is a term I coined for applications that make themselves appear larger (in terms of features) than they really are. How can this be done, you might ask? Or, better yet, why would anyone ever want to do this? For one thing, it is a great way to build an entire application out of a tiny amount of content. This allows small software companies to create very niche-oriented products in a short amount of time. It also allows you to inflate your application's feature list beyond that of your competitors'.

For example, imagine you created a great spell-checker utility and wanted to turn it into what appears to be a real application. By simply adding the standard Windows menu system: **File** (to open and save a word list), **Edit** (to cut/copy/paste words), **Window** (to maintain some child windows), and **Help** (to open a cheesy little help file and an about box), you would have, in effect, already laid the groundwork for an application. Next, add a toolbar and a splash screen and presto! You have "Joe Shmoe's Spell-Checker 1.0 for Windows." Even if you were not going to sell it, making your small utility appear like a whole product will put you in the limelight at your company, big time!

Although that was just a silly little example of UI bulking, don't think it can't be put to some serious use. Take a look at the new Windows 95 shell, for instance. Consider for a moment My Computer, which appears at the top left of the desktop, and the Windows Explorer, which appears on the Start menu. Although they sound like two entirely different things, take a closer look and you will see that, except for the dual-pane view in the Explorer, they are almost exactly alike. As a matter of fact, many of the Windows 95 features that appear on the desktop as separate icons are all just different ways of opening the same thing. (i.e., Recycle Bin, Briefcase, Control Panel, etc.)

| Wrapping It Up |

Obviously, a lot more goes into turning a program into an application than just these things. Nevertheless, it's a good start. In the upcoming chapter we examine the Windows 95 interface guidelines and how they can be used to really add polish to your product. No more fooling around!

CHAPTER THREE

Following Guidelines

The Windows Interface Guidelines are our last great hope, particularly in this era of multimedia. So many of today's new titles deviate from these guidelines and attempt to create their own look and feel. Isn't that just the thing Windows promised to abolish in the first place?

Why did this happen? How could this happen? It appears as though the very thing that promised to deliver us from inconsistency has brought us just that, a complete about-face. (No pun intended.) The craziest thing about all of this is that I've even come across some popular Microsoft products that don't readily conform to their own interface guidelines—the guidelines they created in the first place! Too many times people set out on a journey in search of an answer to a problem and find themselves right back where they started. This phenomenon can be found in just about every facet of modern-day life. In pharmacology, for example, you'd be amazed at just how many medicines have side effects or withdrawal effects causing the very same problem that they were supposed to alleviate in the first place.

Let's take a closer look at why so many programs deviate from these guidelines. At its most basic level, the answer can be broken down into two reasons: ignorance and pride. Those in charge of software design are either completely oblivious to any interface guidelines, or they simply could care less and think that their way of doing things is the only way. No matter how you slice it, by having control of a program's interface we try to personalize it and often times, hoping for our 15 minutes of fame, we let our pride take over.

So who is in charge anyway? Is it a big-talking marketing manager who thinks he is going to be the next Bill Gates? I sure hope not. Is it a geeky programmer who never enjoyed taking a single art class? (You know the type.) Or is it an artsy-fartsy designer who hated mathematics and doesn't even own a computer? If it were your money being spent, would you want any of these people designing your software? I think not.

In light of all this, how can we make sure that our software is well designed? In my opinion, the best answer is to hire people who love science and math, own a computer, and enjoy art as a hobby. These are well-balanced, left brain/right brain kind of people. Otherwise, a group of highly specialized individuals must act as a team and help to balance the unit as a whole when it comes to designing an application's interface. Regardless of which of these two scenarios is used, it is critical that each individual involved in software development be aware and have a good clear understanding of the Windows Interface Guidelines for Software Design. This chapter presents those guidelines in a quick, concise format.

The Windows Interface Guidelines for Software Design is a highly recommended book that no programmer, software designer, or manager of Windows software development should be without. It is available from Microsoft Press at 1-800-MSPRESS.

Concise Windows 95 Interface Guidelines

When your users start up your program for the very first time they will have certain expectations. They will expect your Windows software to look and feel like a Windows application, just as you would expect someone from France to look and speak as a French person. If these visual and interactive expectations are not met, the new user will quickly become frustrated. You'll make inexperienced users feel stupid, and experienced users will think *you're* stupid. That's not a great way to get people to fall in love with your software. Following the Windows guidelines for software design will help keep this from happening.

Design Concepts

Designing for the User

Put the user in the driver's seat...

Long gone are the days of those old menu-driven programs, and I don't mean "menus" in the sense of pull-down or pop-up menus. I'm talking about all those lists of choices that would appear one right after the other in order to navigate to a specific part of a program or to perform some particular task. At any given point in time, nothing could be done except make a choice from a list. Even though you could always go back to the previous menu you never really felt as though you knew where you were. This type of *modality* limited the user's ability to control the program. A *mode* is any situation in which a user is temporarily restricted from an action that would otherwise be readily available. Remember, the user should control the program, not the other way around.

Obviously, in certain cases *modes* cannot be avoided. For example, it would be kind of silly and unnecessary to have the common file dialogs (File Open and File Save) be anything but modal. Because the user explicitly chose to open or save a particular file, and having the option to cancel is clearly defined, there is no need to allow these dialogs to linger around the desktop.

All in all, your software should be more like a car than like a train. In other words, the user is an active participant and not just along for a ride. The user should be able to act and not have to constantly react. By empowering your users, your software will become a tool and not just a program.

Tap into the user's real-world experiences...

Using metaphors to depict the objects in your software is a great way to give instant power to your users. Let's face it, we all come equipped with an amazing amount of knowledge regarding how things work in our real world. Everybody knows that doors can be opened and doors can be shut. By tapping into the real world's human interface, you can bring a whole new level of meaning to the words "easy to use." The file folder is a classic example of this. Without having any previous experience, a new user instantly knows that a folder is a container of other objects.

Maintain a consistent look and feel...

As mentioned before in Chapter One, consistency is crucial for good software design. Not only should your software be consistent in and of itself, but it should also be consistent with the Windows environment. This kind of consistency will allow your users to quickly and easily transfer the knowledge they have already learned from using other Windows applications and, at the same time, provide them with a level of predictability that will make your product appear stable and easy to use.

When things are different for no apparent reason or, worse yet, change from one moment to the next, a sense of sloppiness will prevail. How many cars do you know of that are still being manufactured with a stick shift on the steering column? Even if some drivers preferred this to a standard floor-mounted stick shift, the automobile industry quickly learned that it was better to be consistent.

In a way, consistency is very closely tied to the previously mentioned guideline of tapping into a user's real world experiences. Think about it; by being consistent you are in effect tapping into the user's previous knowledge of the way things should be in a Windows application.

Have mercy on the user...

In real life, we all make mistakes and have the right to change our minds. Likewise, a product should be as forgiving as possible whenever an action can drastically change the state of things. When an action cannot be undone, the user should be forewarned and should, at that point, be able to cancel the action.

A product should also encourage exploration without endangering the user's data. Because most Windows users do not read many manuals and like to learn as they go, it is essential that you design your product to be as safe and forgiving as possible.

Let the user know what's going on...

In my opinion, visual feedback is one of the most satisfying things to design, program, and see. It's one of the few times that the user feels as if the computer is really doing something for him. When a product keeps the user well informed about the status of a process during a time-consuming event it treats the user with respect.

Many different types of user feedback are available to the Windows software designer. Among the more common ones are progress indicators, animated icons, hourglass cursors, status bars, sound, and what I call "ticker text" (text that is continuously updated as new information becomes readily available). An example of ticker text would be a search dialog that displays the current directory while the search is in progress. I'm sure you've seen all these in one form or another.

As a rule of thumb, whenever there is a delay of more than a couple of seconds be sure to let the user know what is going on. At the very least, make use of the hourglass cursor. An interface that is unresponsive for more than a couple of seconds can trigger anxiety in your users or make them feel as though your program is inefficient.

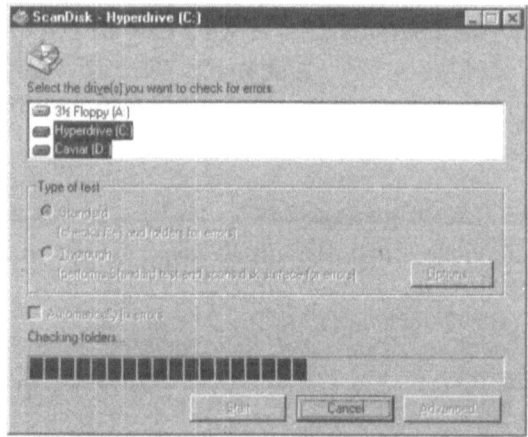

The Windows 95 progress indicator in action.

Care about the way things look...

If you don't care about the way things look then you probably shouldn't have anything to do with designing an interface. The way your software looks will have a huge impact on your users' emotions. Ugly-looking software can depress people just as much as ugly looking things can. Ugly clothes, ugly furniture, and ugly software—they all belong in a basement somewhere in an ugly house.

Again, if you don't care about the way things look, or simply have bad taste, then, for the sake of everyone, let somebody else handle the aesthetic aspects of your software. Even though we all share the same capacity for a sense of beauty, some of us are often too preoccupied to appreciate it. This sense of design is like a muscle, it must be exercised regularly in order to grow strong.

Keep things simple...

I touched on the importance of simplicity in Chapter One, so it should come as no surprise to find out that it is also an integral part of the Windows interface guidelines. Think of simplicity as being the shortest distance between two points. Simplicity is efficiency in its most perfect form. It is clean and offends no one. This is what you should strive for when designing software. It is important to remember, however, that simplicity is not the same thing as being simplistic. You want to design software that is easy to use, not software that insults your users' intelligence.

Test your designs...

Great software design can only come about through the repetitive process of designing, prototyping, and testing. Just as writing a book requires many passes back and forth, using this word and that word, interface design can only be perfected through constant repetition and analysis.

If you recall, in Chapter Two I discussed various design techniques such as side-by-side design and layout comparison. Once you've arrived at an initial design by using either one or both of those techniques, the next logical step is to create a prototype using a rapid application development environment such as Microsoft Visual Basic. Regardless of what development system is chosen, it is important that the programmers do not get in the bad habit of building an application using sloppy prototype code. This happens much more often than you might think.

(For a close look at prototyping with Visual Basic see Chapter Five—Prototyping 101.)

After you have a working prototype, the real fun begins. Your software design is now ready to be introduced to the real world through a process known as *usability testing*. This process can range anywhere from simply showing your colleagues a prototype and asking them what they think, to hiring an expensive firm that specializes in focus groups and having them evaluate the prototype. Although, depending on the size of your company and/or the importance of your project, the process used will vary, conducting some sort of usability test should not be overlooked. This cycle can be repeated as many times as you like, with each iteration moving your product that much closer to perfection.

Data-Centricity

Object-oriented design...

If you recall, Chapter One introduced you to a technique that can be used to help create an object-oriented interface. In this chapter, I discuss some of the reasons why having an object-oriented interface is important and how this all fits in with the Microsoft user interface guidelines.

It is much easier for a user to understand software that is fashioned in an object-oriented manner than it is for her to understand software that is not. For example, it is far more natural to think about your "letter to mom" than it is to think about a word-processing program that opens your "letter to mom." This extra layer of indirection can confuse many users and force them to think in an awkward kind of way. In the "letter to mom" example, the letter is an object, or noun, and what the user chooses to do with that letter is the verb. She may want to spell-check it, change its type size, save it, or print it. This way of thinking is very intuitive and direct. Ultimately, you want your product to look and feel less like a program that works on objects and more like objects that can be worked on by the user. This is what makes an application *data-centric*.

Understanding objects...

It's important that you have a good clear understanding of object-oriented principles if you are to use them effectively in your software designs. To make sure of this, let's take a close look at an automobile in an object-oriented fashion. An automobile is an object and each individual automobile has certain characteristics that make it unique. These characteristics are called *properties*. Properties of an automobile include things such as color, engine size, number of doors, make, and model.

The verbs that can be applied to a particular object are called *methods*. Using the example of an automobile, its methods would include all things that can be done with or done to that automobile. Some such methods include start, accelerate, turn, stop, and wash.

As you build your designs around an object-oriented paradigm, it is important to pay close attention to the *relationships* that exist between your objects. You may have a *collection* of different automobile objects, or, your automobile may be composed of other objects, such as seats. In this case, the automobile object is acting as a *container* for a collection of seat objects which in turn have their own properties and methods.

Windows

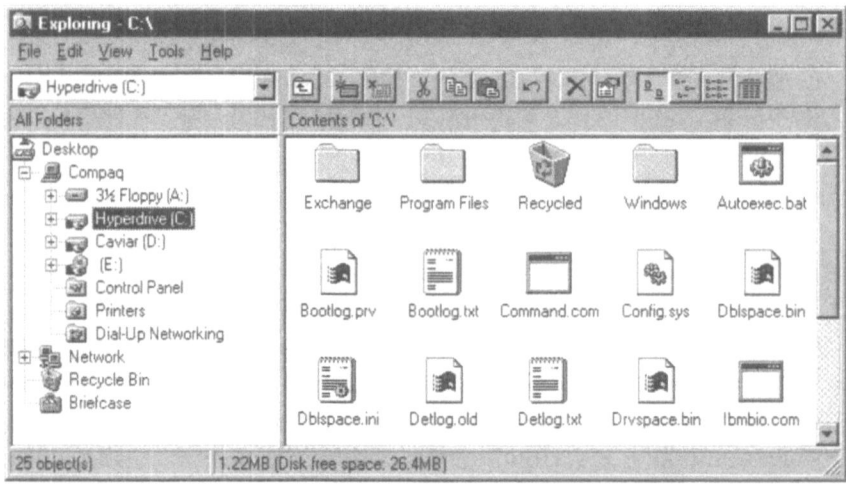

The Windows 95 Explorer window has a little bit of everything.

Anatomy of a Window

This section takes a close look at the details of a window, and the section that follows, **Types of Windows**, describes each of the different types of windows that are available to the software designer, and how and when to use them.

Window frame...

Every window has some type of border or frame around it. The type of frame a window has defines what type of window it is and whether it can be resized. Window frames are available in the following styles: none, fixed single, sizable, fixed dialog, fixed tool window, and sizable tool window. The differences between these styles are discussed in the following section.

A resizable window is said to have *handles* located along its frame. These handles become evident to the user as the mouse cursor is positioned over the frame. By clicking on a frame handle and then dragging the mouse, the user can directly manipulate the window size.

If a window is resizable and has a *status bar* (see the following), a *size grip* should also be present. The size grip is nothing more than a handle that has a permanent visual presence (unlike frame handles that become evident only when the mouse pointer is moved over them) and always appears in the same location (at the bottom-right corner of the window).

Title bar...

The title bar of a window has many purposes: it identifies the window by displaying a title, it displays the name of the current document (if it is a document-based application), it displays a 16 x 16 pixel (16-color) icon (for the application or the current document), and can contain three window manipulation buttons (Minimize, Maximize /Restore, and Close). Also, the user can click and drag the title bar, using his mouse, to move the window to a different location on the desktop, or he can double-click on the title bar to quickly maximize and restore the window.

Window manipulation buttons...

Button	Name	Action
⊟	Minimize	Shrinks the window into a window button.
☐⊡	Maximize/Restore	Toggles the window between maximum and original size.
☒	Close	Closes the window.

Keep in mind that, depending on the type of window, not every one of these features will be enabled in the title bar. For example, if a window is not resizable, the maximize button would be disabled. Likewise, if the window is a dialog box, no 16 x 16 pixel icon would be displayed in the title bar.

Menu bar...

The menu bar, if present, appears directly below the title bar and provides the user with a list of available commands. The individual choices that appear along the menu bar are called *menu titles*. When a specific menu title is chosen, via the mouse or keyboard, a *drop-down menu* containing a list of *menu items* is displayed. For more information on menus and how to use them effectively see the upcoming **Controls—Menus** section.

Toolbars...

Moving down from the top of the window, the toolbar is typically the next interface object; it sits directly below the menu bar. Although a window can have only one visible menu bar at a time, it can have multiple toolbars layered on top of one another. This is particularly relevant when using the in-place activation features of object linking and embedding (see **Object Linking and Embedding—In-Place Activation**).

The toolbar provides a great place for the most commonly used features and commands of your application to reside. Buttons on the toolbar can contain graphics, text, and tool tips (see the upcoming section on **Controls**). Besides making your application more user-friendly, toolbars can add a great deal of aesthetic beauty to your interface. For both reasons, the toolbar has come to be a commonly expected feature.

In the world of successful software design, there are two basic types of toolbar look and feel. The first is like Microsoft Office which sports an intelligent use of space and clean simple graphics. Instead of placing descriptive text on each individual button, tool tips are automatically displayed as the user momentarily hovers the mouse pointer over each button. The other type of toolbar look and feel is much more consumer-oriented and, perhaps, even slightly more friendly in nature. The buttons on this type of toolbar have captions directly below a colorful icon. Some examples of this type of toolbar can be seen in products like Quicken, WordPerfect, and the Lotus Smart Suite.

Scroll bars...

Scroll bars come in two different flavors: horizontal and vertical. Both work in the same way by allowing the user to pan from left to right or up and down, hence seeing what would otherwise not be visible due to lack of space. Scroll bars are dynamic in the sense that they appear and disappear depending on whether they are needed. Whenever a window can be reduced in size or there is not enough screen space, scroll bars serve a vital role by allowing the user to see what would otherwise be hidden or out of view.

Split bars...

Like scroll bars, split bars, or splitters, are also available in either a horizontal or vertical orientation. A split bar allows a user to split the current view into two or to designate how the screen's real estate should be divided between two different panes.

The word processor I am using right now (Microsoft Word) allows me to split my view of this page into two using a horizontal split bar that is located directly above the vertical scroll bar. Instead of having one scrollable view, I can have two, each one capable of showing a different part of the same document. Similarly, the Microsoft Explorer window (shown back on page 42), has a vertical split bar that allows the user to dynamically control the width of the desktop tree (on the left side of the window) versus the width of the contents list (on the right side of the window).

Status bar...

A status bar can appear at the bottom of a window and should only exist in a primary window, not a secondary one. (For information on primary and secondary windows, see the following topic.) A status bar provides a place for a product to communicate to the user. It can be used to display the current state of things (page/record number, keyboard toggles, progress indicator, date, time, etc.), or, to display a verbose description of a selected menu item. A status bar can be broken into multiple sections when displaying more than one piece of information. If a window is resizable, the status bar provides a place for the size grip.

Types of Windows

Application and document windows...

Every application or utility has what is called a *primary window*. The primary window is the main window of an application and appears in the Windows 95 task bar. Typically, the primary window is the first window that comes up after a program has been started (not counting the splash screen). From the primary window, the user is then able to open and close any other *secondary windows*, such as dialog boxes, *document windows* (if it is an MDI application, see the following), and/or tool windows. Primary windows are usually resizable, whereas most secondary windows are not (an exception would be document windows). This is the basic structure of most Windows applications.

An application is said to be document-based when it has the ability to create, save, and open files through the use of the standard File menu (New, Open..., Save, and Save As...). An application can be thought of as being document-based if the data it creates and modifies can be considered to be an object in and of itself. A letter, a spreadsheet, a graph, and a slide presentation are some examples of objects that fit into the document-based (data-centric) design model. Be careful not to confuse an application that simply opens and saves settings (such as a simple loan amortization program) with one that is document-based.

It is important, at this point in time, to distinguish between the two different models of document-based interfaces that are available to the software designer. The *Single Document Window Interface* (SDI) and the *Multiple Document Window Interface* (MDI). Although, in the past (i.e., with Windows 3.1), most document-based applications used an MDI interface, the momentum is now swinging in the direction of SDI. The reasons for this shift in preference can be found by looking at the concepts behind each design model.

An MDI document-based interface contains one primary *parent window* and one or more *child windows*, each of which can have a different document open at any given time. Initially thought of as being a powerful design model, the MDI interface has run into its share of problems. Because users did not easily grasp the concept of overlapping windows, the MDI interface proved to be mediocre at best. Making matters worse, child windows are constrained to the inside of the parent window. In other words, a child window could not be moved around with the freedom of other windows, and, worse yet, if maximized, many users would find themselves hunting for missing windows. Like anything else, the MDI interface does have its advantages and, in many cases, it is still an appropriate design model. SDI, on the other hand, provides a much simpler document-based interface but allows for only one document to be open at a time. However, because the user is able to start up as many instances of an application as he wants (provided there is enough memory), this is hardly a problem.

Regardless of whether it is an MDI or an SDI interface, the document windows themselves should be resizable. Document windows from an MDI application have a much simpler interface than those of an SDI application. Think about it. In the case of an SDI application, the document window and the primary window are one and the same. This means that the document window may also need to have a menu bar, a toolbar, and maybe even a status bar. The MDI document window doesn't need any of those things since its parent has already taken care of all that.

Title bar conventions for document-based applications...

Situation	Title bar icon	Title text
MDI w/ a child window	Application	Application
MDI w/ child maximized	Application	Application - Document
SDI	Document	Document - Application

Tool windows...

Tool windows, or tool boxes, are secondary windows that have a Close button and display their title bar text using a reduced font size. They can either be fixed or resizable and are commonly used as floating toolbars. Tool windows are often designed to be "Always on Top" of other windows, regardless of the current active window. Tool windows do not appear in the Windows 95 task bar.

The Microsoft Paint tool window.

Dialog boxes...

Dialog boxes are secondary windows that allow for communication, or an exchange of information, to take place between the user and the computer. Dialog boxes can be initiated by your software when more information is required from the user before a particular task, such as saving a file, can be carried out. Likewise, the user can also initiate a dialog in order to communicate with the software—for example, setting options or modifying the current page setup. Dialog boxes are not resizable, are typically modal, and do not appear in the Windows 95 task bar.

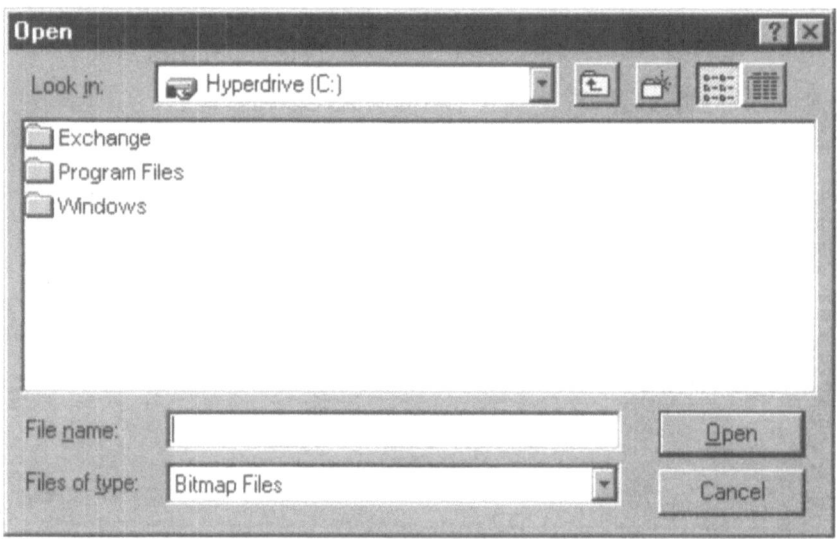

The Windows 95 common file Open dialog.

Menu items and command buttons that lead the user to a dialog box should always be followed by an ellipsis (i.e., Page Setup..., Options..., Save As...). Be sure not to include the ellipsis in the dialog box's title bar text.

Message boxes...

From a designer's point of view, message boxes are one of the easiest windows to implement. All you have to do is decide what type of icon should be used (Critical ⊗, Exclamation ⚠, or Information ⓘ), what the text of the message to the user should be, and which button combination should be displayed (OK, OK/Cancel, Abort/Retry/Ignore, Yes/No, Yes/No/Cancel, or Retry/Cancel). Of these three tasks the most easily overlooked is choosing the appropriate icon. Not doing so can inadvertently scare your users, or, worse yet, not scare them enough.

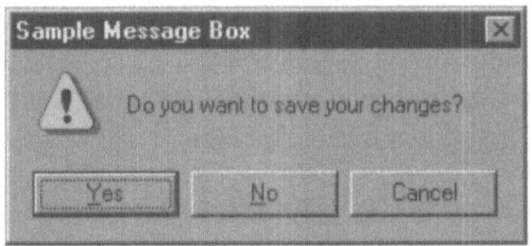

A exclamation type message box with yes, no, and cancel buttons.

A dialog is said to be modal if it restricts the user from an action that would otherwise be readily available. Message boxes are always modal to the current application and, in some cases, can be modal to the entire system. In the latter case, all active applications are suspended until the user responds to the message box.

Real-World Issue:
Message box title bar text...

The text that appears in a message box title should always identify the application or object that displayed the message.

Controls

Types of Controls

Menus...

If you recall, in the previous section, I talked a little bit about menu bars, and how the menus themselves are called *pull-down*, or *drop-down*, menus. These pull-down menus allow an application to present its features using an intuitive list of commands. When a specific menu title is chosen from the menu bar, via the mouse or keyboard, a pull-down menu containing a list of menu items is displayed.

In addition to the pull-down menu, there is another type of menu control, called a *pop-up menu,* which is used extensively throughout Windows 95. Pop-up menus are displayed whenever the user clicks on an object using the right mouse button. The pop-up menu enables the user to directly manipulate an object's properties and/or choose one of its available commands. (see **Design Concepts—Data Centricity**)

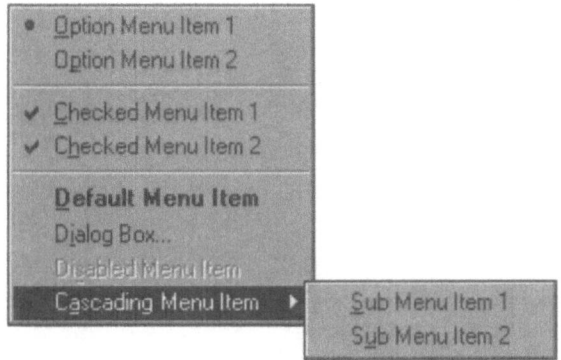

Whether you're designing a pull-down or a pop-up menu, there are a number of different types of menu items from which you can choose.

It is critical that your application's menu structure conform with other Windows applications. By simply looking at a menu bar and browsing through its pull-down menus, it is easy to determine whether a product was properly designed. Many times I've come across applications that were ported from another platform and still kept using their old, inconsistent menu structure, and other times I've seen menus that were incorrectly designed from the beginning.

You can use this table as a guide to help you design your menus...

Menu	Item	Shortcut	Description
File	New	Ctrl+N	Starts a new document.
	Open...	Ctrl+O	Opens the file open dialog.
	Save	Ctrl+S	Saves the current document.
	Save As...		Saves, using a new file name.
	_____		*separator bar*
	Print...	Ctrl+P	Opens the print dialog box.

	Print Preview		Prints document to the screen.
	Page Setup...		Opens a document setup dialog.
	———————		*separator bar*
	recent file list		*Lists the four most recently used files.*
	———————		*separator bar*
	Exit	Alt+F4	Closes the application.
Edit	Undo	Ctrl+Z	Undoes the previous edit command.
	———————		*separator bar*
	Cut	Ctrl+X	Moves selection to clipboard.
	Copy	Ctrl+C	Copies selection to clipboard.
	Paste	Ctrl+V	Pastes clipboard data to cursor.
	Paste Special...		Displays OLE paste object dialog.
	Clear	Del	Clears current selection.
	Select All	Ctrl+A	Selects all items in the current object.
	———————		*separator bar*
	Find...	Ctrl+F	Displays a find dialog.
	Find Next	F3	Repeats the previous search.
	Replace...	Ctrl+H	Opens search and replace dialog.
	———————		*separator bar*
	Links...		Displays a dialog showing all OLE links.
	Insert Object...		Displays an insert object dialog box.
	selected OLE object		Allows editing and opening of a selected object from within OLE container application.

<u>V</u>iew	*application specific menu items*		The View menu can contain any commands that affect how data in the current document is viewed.
	————		*separator bar*
	<u>T</u>oolbar		Check box to show/hide a toolbar.
	<u>S</u>tatus Bar		Check box to show/hide a status bar.
	————		*separator bar*
	<u>O</u>ptions...		Dialog for application-specific options.
product specific menus			Application-specific menus are typically put between the View menu and the Window menu.
<u>W</u>indow *MDI only*	<u>T</u>ile	Shft-F5	Arranges child windows like tiles, within the MDI workspace.
	<u>C</u>ascade		Puts windows on top of each other.
	Arrange <u>I</u>cons		Rearranges minimized child windows.
	————		*separator bar*
	window list		List of open child windows.
<u>H</u>elp	<u>H</u>elp Topics		Opens the help topics dialog.
	What's This?		Invokes the help cursor.
	————		*separator bar*
	<u>A</u>bout...		Displays about box.

Obviously, not all of these menu items will apply to your application. You should, however, be able to get a good idea of how and where things should appear. (For more information on the Edit menu's Paste Special..., Links..., and Object menu items, see the next section on **Object Linking and Embedding.**)

Real-World Issue:
When designing a new application, where is the best place to start?

Designing the menus first is a great way to make sure everything will fit together as planned.

Buttons...

Buttons are an integral part of our daily lives and are, perhaps, the most widely used interface object in the world. Just think about your car's dashboard, your microwave oven, or your TV's remote control. I bet there are probably more buttons on any one of those than on most computer screens.

There are four basic kinds of buttons in Windows: command buttons, picture buttons, check boxes, and option (radio) buttons. Although the first three can be used by themselves, option buttons cannot. They should only be used in groups of two or more.

Command buttons are what most people think of when they hear the word "button"—as long as you're not talking to a tailor. Command buttons are raised, three-dimensional rectangles and typically have a word or two for a caption. Command buttons allow a user to take control, or, better yet, take command, of an application. Command buttons provide a familiar response mechanism, regardless of the user's level of computer literacy.

A command button can be designed as a default button or a cancel button. The default button is the button the user is expected to choose most often, and it is automatically clicked if the user presses the Enter key. The cancel button, which gives the user a way out of a dialog, is clicked when the Escape key is pressed. The default button is designated with a darker border than the other buttons. There can only be one default and one cancel button per dialog.

As I said before, command buttons that lead the user to a dialog box should always have their caption be followed by an ellipsis (e.g., Page Setup..., Options..., Save As...). Remember not to include the ellipsis in the dialog box's title bar text.

For all intents and purposes, **picture buttons** behave much in the same way as command buttons, with two exceptions: there is typically no default button and, if on a toolbar, they do not receive focus from the tab key. Picture buttons can also be designed to have both an up and a down state, hence, behaving just like a check box or an option button—for this reason they are sometimes called "sticky buttons." (See the following for more information on check boxes and option buttons.)

Even though picture buttons are most commonly used in toolbars and tool windows, they can make quite attractive command buttons.

Picture buttons can have a caption along with their picture. It all depends on the particular style of the interface. When picture buttons do not have descriptive text, tool tips should be used. A tool tip is pop-up text that appears automatically when the mouse pointer is momentarily positioned over a button and explains the function of the button.

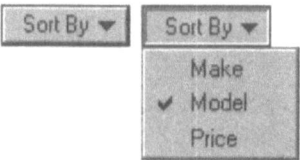

Combining a picture button with a pop-up menu gives you what is sometimes called a **menu button**. A menu button can be easily identified by a right-justified down arrow. Notice how a menu button toggles between an up and a down state. Using menu buttons can help you reduce screen clutter and give your application a clean and intelligent feel.

☑ Contribute to campaign fund?

Check boxes are simply buttons that can be either on or off. A check box's value does not affect the values of other check boxes—unlike option buttons (see the following). Check boxes are commonly found in dialog boxes.

A multistate check box is a check box that toggles between various states—although more than three states is not recommended. The Microsoft Backup utility uses multistate check boxes to indicate whether only some (using a gray check mark) or all (using a black check mark) of a directory folder has been selected for backup.

Option buttons work together in groups of two or more. They are often called radio buttons because when one is on, the others are off—much like an old radio's station buttons. More often than not, the first option button in a group is usually the one that is on by default. If you are designing a dialog box that requires more than one group of option buttons, you will need to use group boxes. Group boxes are described in the following.

Real-World Issue:
When two option buttons equal one check box...

If space is tight and you're using two option buttons to represent a Boolean condition (i.e., Yes/No, On/Off, True/False), consider using one check box instead.

Text fields...

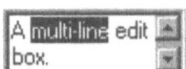

Text fields provide the user with the ability to enter and edit text. The **edit box** is the simplest kind of text field. Thanks to Windows 95, all edit boxes now provide full clipboard support via the right mouse button. Edit boxes can either be multi-line or single-line. A multi-line edit box allows the user to enter carriage returns in the text. Because the text may not all fit on one line, edit boxes provide full scroll bar support. Edit boxes can also be designed to accept only certain kinds of data, such as numeric or fixed-format (e.g., a zip code).

If an edit box only accepts numeric data, a **spin box** may be a better alternative. The spin box allows the user to increment and decrement the value of the edit box using the mouse.

In addition to letting the user simply enter and edit text, the **rich text box** also provides advanced formatting features. Selected text can be formatted using different fonts and attributes, such as bold, italic, and underline. In addition, the rich text box control can read and write rich text format (RTF) files. Think of the rich text box control almost as a tiny word processor.

A **combo box** is an edit box that has been combined with a list box or a drop-down list box, hence the name "combo." The user can use do one of two things with a combo box: she can type her own response into the edit box portion, or she can select a response from a list of available choices in the list box portion. If appropriate, the user's response can then be added, by the programmer, to the list of available choices.

List boxes...

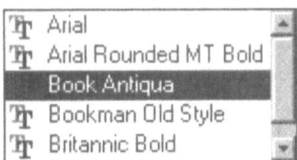

The **list box** is used to provide the user with a large number of choices using a limited amount of space. Using a vertical scroll bar, the user is able move up and down through the list of items. Similarly, a list box can also have a horizontal scroll bar. This allows the user to pan from left to right and see any items that exceed the width of the list box. Typically, however, a list box should be wide enough to accommodate the width of all items in the list.

The items in the list box can be thought of as either a list of check boxes or a list of option buttons. In the latter case, a list of option buttons, the list box is said to be a single-select list box. In other words, only one of the many choices can be selected at any given time. A multi-select list box, on the other hand, behaves just as a list of check boxes would, where individual items can be toggled between a selected and deselected state.

Multi-select list boxes come in two flavors: simple or extended. A simple multi-select list box allows the user to toggle the state of an item by simply clicking on it with the mouse. One click selects the item, another deselects it, just as with a check box.

An extended multi-select list box supports a more powerful (albeit less intuitive) keyboard interface. The user can extend the current selection by holding down the shift key and clicking the mouse on another item in the list, or by using the arrow keys to select more items. This will extend the selection from the previously selected item to the newly selected item. To select items in a noncontiguous manner, the user must hold down the Ctrl key while clicking on items in the list. Holding down the Ctrl key temporarily turns an extended multi-select list box into a simple multi-select list box.

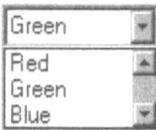

If you thought the list box saved space on the screen, wait until you see a **drop-down list box**! Just as with a single-select list box, the drop-down list box allows the user to choose one item from a list of many. The big difference is that the drop-down list box only displays the one selected item. The list of choices can be instantly shown, or hidden, by clicking on the drop-down list box's down arrow button. Note how the drop-down list box is almost identical to the drop-down combo box (discussed before) with the exception that the user cannot enter a value that is not already in the list.

Description	Code
▷ Cholera	001
▷ Due to Vibrio cholerae	001.0
▷ Due to Vibrio cholerae el tor	001.1
▷ Cholera, unspecified	001.9
▷ Typhoid and paratyphoid fevers	002
▷ Typhoid fever	002.0

Think of the **list view** control as a list box that allows the user to customize the way in which items are displayed and/or sorted. The list view control is new for Windows 95 and is used extensively throughout the entire Windows 95 shell.

Any window that uses a list view control should allow the user to modify the way in which the data is displayed. This can be done by using a View menu. The View menu should appear both in the menu bar and as a pop-up menu, via the right mouse button.

The list view control allows the user to organize list items into one of four different views: large icons, small icons, list, and report (or details). When viewing by large icons (32 x 32 pixels) or by small icons (16 x 16 pixels), the user can organize the individual items in any way he chooses (by dragging and dropping with a mouse) or automatically sort them using the View menu. Each list item is represented by both an icon and a text label.

Viewing by list is very similar to viewing by small icons in that each list item is represented by a small icon and a label, which appears to the right of the icon. The list items, however, are always arranged into vertical columns.

The report view can be used to provide additional information about each list item. In this view, list items appear in columns with the leftmost column containing the small icon and text label. Additional columns can be added to display any extra information that is pertinent to each list item. To accommodate screen real estate, column headings can be instantly resized and/or scrolled horizontally. In addition, the report view allows the user to quickly re-sort the list by simply clicking on a column heading. One click sorts the items into ascending order, another reverses the sort into descending order.

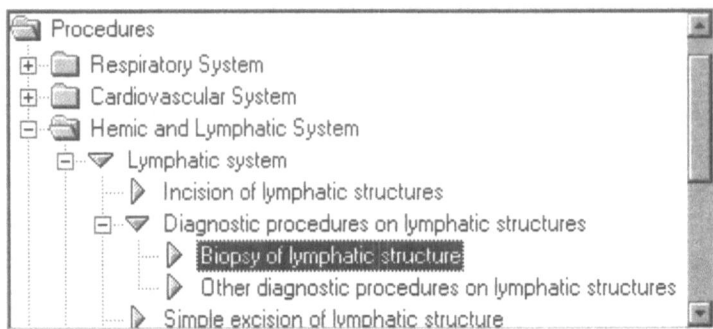

Use the **tree view** control to display a hierarchical list of items. This control is also new for Windows 95 and is used extensively throughout the Windows 95 shell (e.g., Windows Explorer).

The look and feel of the tree view control can be customized to your particular needs. In addition to having a text label, each item in a tree view can be designated with a plus/minus box, an icon, and/or tree lines (see the lines in the preceding picture). List items that have subitems can be expanded and collapsed, and, are typically indicated by a plus/minus box. Each tree view item can have up to two icons—one for its expanded and one for its collapsed state. The user is able to expand and collapse individual nodes by clicking on the plus/minus box, double-clicking on the text label, or pressing the Enter key.

Other controls...

Label Control

Because not every control provides its own text label, the simple **label control** can be quite useful. Text that is displayed next to a control provides the user with a prompt. This prompt is what gives the user the ability to comprehend the purpose of a control. Although many controls include a caption (e.g., check boxes, option buttons, command buttons), there are quite a few that don't (e.g., edit boxes, combo boxes, list boxes).

Group boxes allow you to group related controls together, providing your interface with a higher level of clarity. A group box does not do anything but act as a container for other objects and provide a caption that best describes the group.

The **progress indicator**, or progress bar, control should be used whenever there is a delay (in system response) of more than a couple of seconds. This control provides the user with a sense of security, and keeps him well informed of the status of a process. The progress indicator is typically piggybacked with a label control. The accompanying label control can be used to display what percentage of the job has been completed or a more descriptive status report.

As a rule of thumb, make sure that the width of your progress indicator is at least twelve (12) times larger than its height. This allows for a good chunk size.

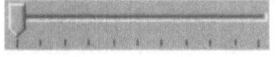

The **slider** control allows the user to specify a value within a range. It can be used in both a horizontal and vertical orientation. (Before Windows 95, the horizontal scroll bar was often used as a slider.) Each slider control can have a minimum and a maximum value, a value indicating how often tick marks should appear, and a large and small change value. The large change value determines the number of ticks the slider will move when the user presses the PageUp/PageDn keys or when the mouse is clicked to the left or right of the slider. Similarly, the small change value determines the amount by which the slider will move when the user presses the left or right arrow keys or drags the slider with the mouse.

Similar to the group box, the **tab** control provides the software designer with another mechanism through which related objects can be logically grouped. The tab control also helps to make the most out of a finite amount of screen space by organizing your interface into pages. If you're looking to add some pizzazz, you can use the tab control with images. Images can appear to the left of each page's caption.

When designing a dialog that uses tabs, be sure not to include the dialog's buttons (e.g., OK, Cancel, Apply) in the tab control itself. Only buttons that relate to each specific page should appear within those pages.

As mentioned before, the **tool tip** control is a great way for your software to teach the user. Think of the tool tip as a way of annotating your interface. Whenever there is an object that needs a little bit of elaboration (e.g., toolbar buttons), throw in a tool tip˝!

Object Linking and Embedding (OLE)

If you ask most Windows 95 users exactly what is object linking and embedding (OLE), you probably won't get much of an answer. This is not to say, however, that they have never used it, quite the contrary. To the user, understanding OLE is not nearly as important as using it. To the software designer, it's the complete opposite.

In a nutshell, object linking and embedding is the means by which two different applications share their objects and/or functionality with each other. In other words, an application can either share its objects and functionality (acting as a server) with other OLE applications, or it can use the objects and functionality provided by other OLE applications (acting as a container). The extent to which both of these things are done varies from one product to the next.

The Object in OLE

In order for a product to have a great interface, it is essential that object-oriented design principles be followed. Nowhere is this more important than it is with respect to object linking and embedding. Just look at the name. The object in OLE comes first, as it should in your software design. An application that has been designed with data-centricity in mind will lend itself well to the concepts behind OLE. (see **Design Concepts—Data-Centricity**) Because a data-centric interface is designed with objects in mind, thinking of ways in which other applications may be able to use those objects is much easier. When it comes to OLE, it's all in the data, stupid!

Linking

The linking part of object linking and embedding allows an application to include another application's data, or a part of that data, within its own document. The big thing to keep in mind here is that the object itself was created and saved by the other application; its data physically resides in a different file. This is an extremely powerful feature for the user. For example, instead of maintaining separate copies of a logo in every company letter, the same original logo file can be used. Later on, if the logo is changed to a different color, the change will automatically be reflected in every letter that is linked to the logo file.

Using the Edit menu (or an Insert menu), the user should be able to link object data in much the same way she uses the clipboard—via a "Paste Special" or an "Object..." menu item. The linked data can then be edited from the parent (or server) application, or from within the container application if In-Place Activation is supported (see the following).

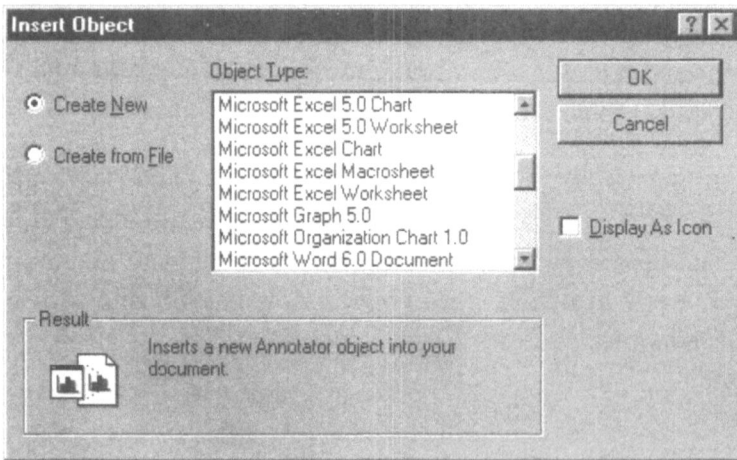

The Insert Object dialog box.

Embedding

The embedding of object linking and embedding is not too different from linking, except that, when an object is embedded, it is saved within the container application's document, whereas, when an object is linked, it is still being saved by the parent application. Only a link to the object is saved within the container application's document. When data is *embedded* within a document, it can not be opened as a separate file using the parent application. It can, however, be opened and edited from within the container application. Double-clicking on the embedded object should open the object's parent application, preferably via In-Place Activation (see the next subsection).

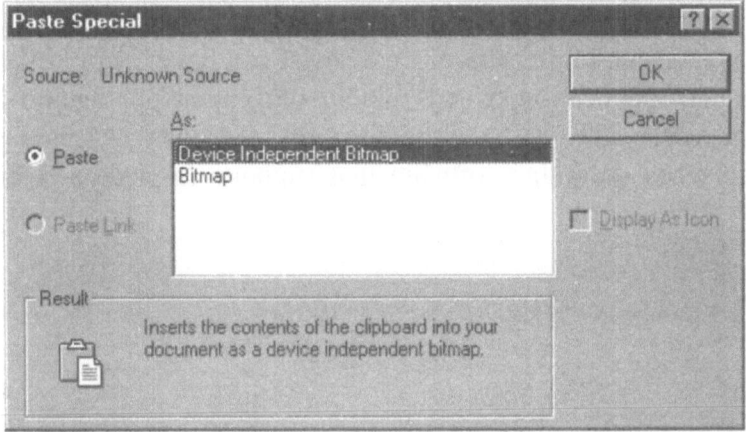

The Paste Special dialog box.

In-Place Activation

The user should always be able to edit any linked or embedded data using the application that was originally used to create that data (the parent application). In the case of linking, the user can directly open the file from within the parent application. When data is embedded, the user simply double-clicks on the object within the container application to open the parent application. It is at this point that the concept of In-Place Activation comes into play. Once an object is double-clicked, or activated, one of two things should happen: either the object's parent application is started up in a separate window, or, preferably, the parent application is melded with the current window (the container application). In other words, the container application's menu and toolbars are dynamically altered to reflect those of the parent application's—all within the same window!

As you can see, when dealing with OLE and in-place activation, issues arise regarding menu and toolbar negotiation. Should the object's toolbar replace the container's toolbar or simply be appended underneath it? Because the user must still have control over the container application, where should the parent application's menus be displayed? These are the kinds of questions that must be answered when designing software that supports in-place activation.

The Windows 95 Environment

The Desktop

The desktop metaphor provides the user with a home base, or starting point. It is from here that all tasks originate. There are three basic ways to start an application in Windows 95, and all of them begin with the desktop. The user can start an application using the taskbar (described in the following), the "My Computer" icon (or Windows Explorer), or directly from the desktop (via a shortcut). This redundancy maximizes the user's ability to quickly locate applications and/or documents.

The desktop is a fully customizable workspace that gives the user complete control over how things should be displayed and organized. A typical Windows 95 desktop will have a basic set of icons representing the computer, any existing network connections, a trash can (for holding deleted files), a universal in/out box (for email, faxes, etc.), and a briefcase (for bringing work home, yuck). In addition, each individual user may have a variety of other icons that appear on the desktop. These additional icons are used to quickly access commonly used objects, such as applications, documents, and printers. In most cases, these icons represent *short cuts*, and are easily distinguished by the ⏎ arrow along their bottom left-hand corner. A short cut, or alias, is simply a file that points to another file or object. If you took a look behind the scenes, you'd quickly realize that most of the icons on the desktop are simply short cuts located in the Windows\Desktop directory.

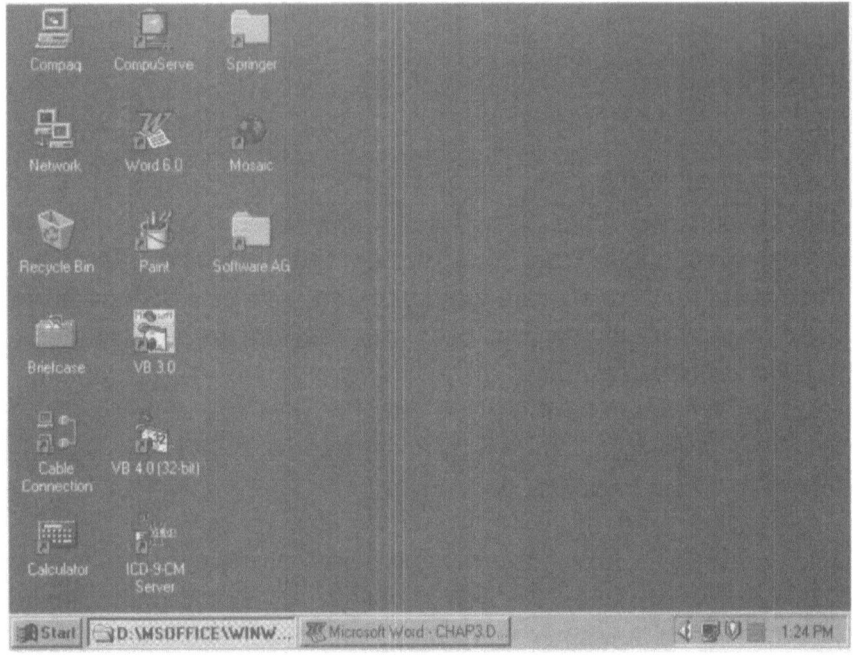

My Desktop.

The Taskbar

The taskbar is typically located along the bottom of the desktop, but can be moved to the top, left, or right side of the screen. The now famous Start button resides on the taskbar. The Start button allows the user to locate applications and documents with unparalleled speed via a simple and effective cascading menu. This one button has single-handedly replaced the entire Windows 3.1 Program Manager.

In addition to the Start button, the taskbar also provides a place for window buttons to reside. Window buttons allow the user to switch between open applications as easily as switching between channels on a television set.

The remaining space of the taskbar is used for displaying the current time and any status notification utilities that may be installed on the system. Status notification utilities allow the user to monitor and, in some cases, modify the current state of the system (e.g., remaining memory, volume settings, video resolution, or incoming mail).

Icons

You just can't get away from them. They're all over the place! Some good, some bad, and some just plain horrible. Icons are here to stay, and are, by far, the most visible aspect of any Windows software product. And now, thanks to Windows 95, our jobs have just gotten a little bit harder with respect to icon design. The software designer must now provide three different kinds of icons for both the application itself and for any document files that may exist. In addition to the standard 32 x 32 pixel (16-color) icon from Windows 3.1, a small 16 x 16 pixel (16-color) icon should also be provided. Otherwise, Windows 95 will scale down the 32 x 32 icon into a homely looking 16 x 16 pixel rendition. To make matters worse, users of Microsoft Plus may expect to see larger 48 x 48 pixel (256 color) icons. In addition to being used by the Windows 95 shell, small icons can also be used within your product's interface (e.g., toolbar buttons, tree view controls, or list view controls)″.

A 48 x 48, 32 x 32, and 16 x 16 icon should be provided for both the application and its documents.

In reality, you don't have to provide anything other than the standard 32 x 32 pixel icons, as long as you don't mind having your
small icons look a little weird. Keep this in mind: as a rule of
thumb, the more complicated and intricate a 32 x 32 pixel icon is,
the worse the 16 x 16 scaled down version will appear. As for the
larger 48 x 48 pixel icons, have no fear, not too many applications
tend to include them (as of yet). In order to be able to view large
icons, the user must have Microsoft Plus installed. So don't worry
if you can't fit them into your release schedule. (For a look at some
tips on good icon design, see Chapter One, **Off to a Great Start—
Aesthetics**.)

Windows

The Windows 95 shell is made up of many items, including the
Desktop, Taskbar, Control Panel, and a variety of windows. The
windows are typically represented by icons on the desktop (e.g.,
My Computer, Network Neighborhood, and Recycle Bin), or by
items on the Start menu (e.g., Control Panel, Windows Explorer).
In this section we take a close look at the various windows that
make up the Windows 95 shell and just how closely related they
are to each other.

Hierarchy...

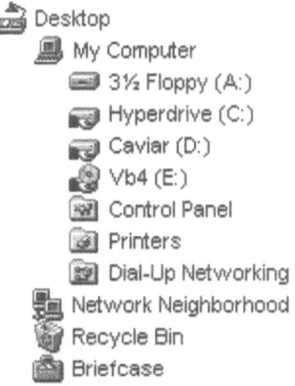

You really can't talk about the windows that make up the Windows 95 shell without first mentioning the hierarchy of objects in Windows 95. The Windows 95 shell is an entirely new interface, not just a simple redesign of Windows 3.1. A lot of thought was put into the shell, particularly as to how items are organized and how they relate to one another. At the topmost level is the desktop. The desktop, as described earlier, envelops the entire Windows 95 shell. The items directly below the desktop constitute the various windows that make up the Windows 95 shell. Each of these items can be browsed using two different windows: My Computer and Windows Explorer. These two windows, as you will soon see, are very similar in design.

Windows...

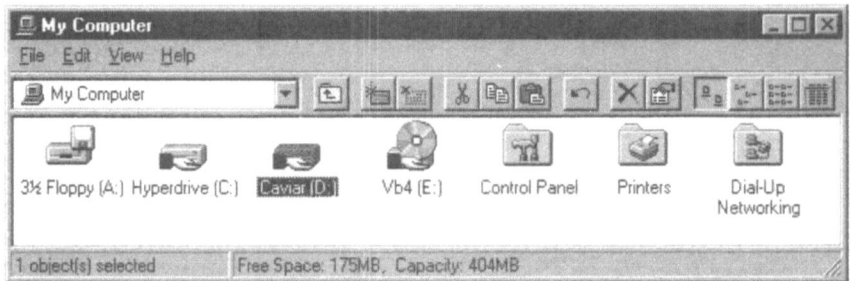

The **My Computer** icon, which typically appears on the top left-hand corner of the desktop, represents the user's physical computer. My Computer allows the user to browse online storage devices, open the Control Panel, and maintain a list of printers. The My Computer window utilizes a single list view control for displaying information to the user. If you recall from page 62, the list view control allows the user to list items using four different views: large icons, small icons, list, and details. All of these views are available from My Computer.

The items that are displayed within the list view portion of My Computer are all part of the Windows 95 hierarchy. This hierarchy is key when it comes to understanding the Windows 95 interface. My Computer allows the user to navigate through this hierarchy in either a sequential or a direct manner. To move further down into the hierarchy, the user can simply double-click on an item in the list view control. This will move her down, sequentially, one level at a time. To move up a level, the user can use the toolbar's drop-down list box to directly jump to another part of the hierarchy, or click on the "Up one level" button that appears to the right of it.

Users have the choice of using a single window or multiple window display when using My Computer. This is an option that can be set from the View menu. When browsing items using only one window, the same list view control is continuously updated as the user moves up and down the hierarchy. Using separate windows causes a new window to be opened each time the user moves to a different location in the hierarchy.

My Computer is a prime example of an object-oriented interface. All the items that appear inside this window are representations of physical objects (metaphors). If the user clicks the right mouse button on one of these objects, a context-sensitive pop-up menu is displayed. The pop-up menu contains a list of commands that are pertinent to that object. The My Computer window is a shell in and of itself. It provides all the necessary commands and features needed to use the Windows 95 operating system.

When it comes to navigating the Windows 95 hierarchy the **Windows Explorer**, without a doubt, takes the cake (see page 42 for a picture). Users of the old File Manager will find a comfortable and familiar interface when using the Explorer. Think of the Explorer as another way of looking at My Computer. For this reason, it's no wonder why "Explore" is one of the verbs that appears in My Computer's pop-up menu when the user right-clicks on its icon. In this case, the Explore command would open an instance of the Windows Explorer entitled "Exploring - My Computer."

To efficiently display a hierarchy, the Windows Explorer uses a tree view control in conjunction with a list view control. Whatever is selected on the left side of the window (using the tree view) will determine what is displayed on the right side of the window (in the list view control). With the Explorer, copying or moving files from one folder to the next can be easily accomplished using a single window because the entire hierarchy is always displayed. With My Computer, the only way to copy and move folders, using a single window, would be to use the clipboard's cut, copy, and paste commands.

The **Network Neighborhood** can be viewed using either My Computer or the Windows Explorer. The Network Neighborhood allows the user to browse and work with networked drives, networked printers, and any existing Windows 95, NT, or Windows for Workgroups peer-to-peer network connections. Windows 95 allows a user to share his or her resources with other users on the network; this is called peer-to-peer networking. In other words, a Windows 95 computer can allow others to access its hard drives, printers, or any other online devices. These resources can be shared using one of two methods: share-level access or user-level access. With share-level access, the user specifies exactly which devices are to be shared. With user-level access, the user creates a list of individuals or groups of individuals who may access the shared resources.

The **Recycle Bin** is a collection of all the recycled directories on a system. Every hard drive is given a designated recycled directory by Windows 95. When a user deletes a file, the file is first moved into its drive's recycled directory. To permanently remove a file, the Recycle Bin must be emptied using the File menu's Empty Recycle Bin command. Once the Recycle Bin has been emptied, files are permanently deleted from every drive's recycled directory. Windows 95 allows you to specify the percentage of space that should be reserved on each drive for recycled files (10%, by default). Just as all other items in the hierarchy, the Recycle Bin can be viewed using either My Computer or the Windows Explorer.

The **Control Panel** allows the user to specify custom settings that alter the way in which hardware devices and system software operate within the Windows 95 environment. The control panel also provides a central location from which to install and remove software, and Plug and Play-compatible hardware. When the user opens the control panel, using My Computer or the Windows Explorer, all the CPL files (*.CPL) that exist in the Windows\System directory are displayed.

A control panel item is a dynamic link library (DLL) that has a CPL extension. If you're designing a control panel item, you'll probably want to use a tabbed property sheet in your window's interface. Or, you may simply want to add a new property sheet page to one of the existing control panel items.

In addition to the various windows described, the user's system may contain a **Briefcase**. In order to use a briefcase, the user must first have installed the portable enhancement features of Windows 95. Having a briefcase facilitates the user's ability to synchronize documents on two different computers (typically a desktop computer and a portable computer). The user must first copy any shared documents into the portable computer's briefcase directory. To do this, both computers must be connected over a network or have a direct-cable connection (with a parallel or serial cable).

Later on, after changes have been made to some of the documents, the user can simply reconnect the two computers and then, using the briefcase, automatically update both machines. This ensures that both computers have the latest version of any documents that exist on both computers and could have been modified by either one.

Installation

Whether you're distributing an application on floppy disks or a CD-ROM, you'll need a good installation program. Nowadays most software companies purchase their installation software, instead of writing it from scratch. There are quite a few different vendors offering installation programs. At the end of this section, I'll recommend one to you. But first, let's discuss some of the necessary features that an installation package must have.

The user should be able to start the installation process using the Control Panel's Add/Remove Programs feature, or by directly running the SETUP.EXE or INSTALL.EXE program using the Start menu's Run command. Prior to Microsoft's adoption of the word *Setup* most companies used the word *Install*. Which one of these two names you choose is entirely up to you.

Regardless of what you call it, the installation software you choose should have, at a minimum, the following features:

- Your installation software should allow you to custom-tailor the look and feel of your installation by providing you with custom dialog boxes, background effects, progress indicators, and the ability to add your own graphics. I'm sure you've seen it before, that famous blue to black faded background that gets used all the time. What if the blue clashes with your company logo? I hope that your installation software will let you select a different background color.

- Your installation software should ask the user whether your product should be added to the taskbar's Start menu or if a shortcut icon should be added to the desktop.

- Your installation software should provide full Registry (see next topic) support and allow you to register icons, any program-specific settings, and/or OLE object references. The ability to modify system files (e.g., autoexec.bat, config.sys, or INI files) is an important feature that should not be sacrificed.

- The ability to create an installation log file is an extremely useful feature to the user. This allows the user to see exactly what went on during the installation process and is an essential part of program removal.

- If you're planning on using the "Designed for Microsoft Windows 95" logo, you'll have to provide an uninstaller. An uninstaller allows the user to remove your program in its entirety without having to go around scrounging for files. The only time a file should not be removed is if it is a document or data file created by the user or a shared system file that is still in use by another installed application. (Windows 95 keeps track of shared files using a reference count. A file's reference count is incremented or decremented during its installation and subsequent removal.)

- Your installation program must provide the ability to compare file versions in order to prevent the unintentional overwriting of a newer file with an older one. This is especially critical when installing shared, or common, files into the user's Windows\System directory.

- The ability to compress files in order to reduce the number of disks that would otherwise be required to distribute your application is another function that you should look for in an installation program. In addition, your installation program should be able to split larger files into chunks that span multiple disks.

I've tried many installation programs, such as InstallShield, Install-It!, Microsoft's VB Setup Wizard, and the WISE Installer. The latter is, in my opinion, the best of them, by far. It has everything you could ever ask for in an installation program. The folks over at Great Lakes Business Solutions should be proud of their work. The WISE Installer provides all the features just described, plus a whole lot more. Not only is it extremely easy to use, it also can be as powerful as you need it to be. [For more information, call (800) 554-8565 or use http://www.glbs.com.]

Using the Registry

Windows 95 removes the need to have separate initialization files, otherwise known as INI files. Instead of using INI files, all applications should now use the registry. The registry acts as a global repository for all application-specific configuration settings. The registry itself is a file (REG.DAT) that is organized into a hierarchical list.

There are advantages and disadvantages to using the registry. On the plus side, users won't have tons of INI files floating around everywhere they look—provided they didn't upgrade from Windows 3.1. On the down side, system integrity is a bit more vulnerable; things can get pretty messy if something happens to the registry file.

The registry file can be directly modified using the Registry Editor (REGEDIT.EXE), which is included with Windows 95. However, the registry is not meant to be modified by the average user. More often than not, the registry is modified during the installation process. This allows an application to have things such as its icons, default path name, and/or any file types registered ahead of time, before the application is ever started. It is also not uncommon for the registry to be modified directly by an application. For example, an application may want to keep a list of its most recently used data files, or whether the user wants a "Tip of the Day" window to be displayed each time the program is run. (It is important that your uninstaller remove any registry entries that were made during the installation process or by your application itself.)

A Word About Windows NT

Microsoft Windows NT 3.51

Users of Windows NT 3.51 and Windows NT Server 3.51 will be glad to hear that they, too, can expect to see applications that have the Windows 95 look and feel. Support for the new Windows 95 controls is provided via the COMCTL32.DLL dynamic-link library. This allows a Windows NT application to use the new Windows 95 controls (e.g., tree view, list view, tabs, progress indicators). However, there are still a few areas of difference between the two interfaces. If you're designing software specifically for Windows NT you should keep the following points in mind:

- Window elements (e.g., minimize, maximize, and close buttons) still look and behave as they did in Windows 3.1.

- The Program Manager and File Manager are still the primary means by which the user launches applications and manages files. In other words, the new Windows 95 shell is not yet available.

- The common file dialogs (i.e., Open, Save, and Save As) still have the Windows 3.1 look and feel.

- There is no way to add and remove programs from the control panel as in Windows 95. Uninstallers should be added to the application's Program Manager group.

- The Registry supports application-specific entries, file commands, shell creation, shell extenders, sound events, and the QuickView command.

- Pen support is not available.

The Windows 95 Logo Program

Think of the Windows 95 logo requirements as a true test for your software design skills. To see whether your software makes the grade, you'll have to submit a final copy to VeriTest (Microsoft's designated testing partner). One thing you should know, however, is that Professor Microsoft is one tough cookie. If your software passes, you'll have a lot to be proud of and celebrate. If it doesn't, then it's going to cost you.

Long gone are the days of simply filling out a long and tedious questionnaire and then, providing all went well, getting to use the Windows logo for free. Now you must have your software tested to see if it meets the compatibility requirements and, perhaps, retested. And, it costs somewhere around $600 for testing and $200 for a retest. Can you believe it? Nevertheless, having the "Designed for Microsoft Windows 95" logo is an obvious status symbol, and one that can help boost sales.

The "Designed for Microsoft Windows 95" logo.

[To find out more about logo testing contact the Microsoft Logo Department at (206) 936-2880 or VeriTest at (310) 450-0062.]

Compatibility with...

So here they are, the Windows 95 software compatibility requirements. These are the factors by which your software will be tested in order to use the logo. The first five requirements are for all applications. The last three apply only to document-based applications.

32-bit compatibility...

First and foremost, your application must be a true Win32 executable. That is, your code must be compiled using a 32-bit compiler that generates an executable of the Portable Executable (PE) format (this format was introduced by Windows NT). You can call 16-bit dynamic-link libraries as long as most of your code is 32-bit. (Calling 16-bit code from a 32-bit application is done using a *thunking,* or translation, mechanism.)

Windows 95 look and feel...

Next, your application must have the Windows 95 look and feel to be considered truly Windows 95-compatible. This can be accomplished by using the controls described in the previous section as well as by using the right mouse button to display context-sensitive pop-up menus, where applicable.

In addition, your application should have a robust installation program that makes use of the Registry (not the WIN.INI or SYSTEM.INI files) and registers both 16 x 16 and 32 x 32 pixel icons for all related files. Your installation program should also provide the user with the ability to uninstall your software. Just as with Windows 3.1, all shared system files should be installed in the user's Windows\System directory using a version check to prevent the overwriting of newer files. Windows 95 keeps track of shared system files by maintaining a reference count. Your installer and uninstaller must increment and decrement these reference counts accordingly, and not inadvertently remove a file that is still required by another installed application.

If your application works with files, you should be using the Windows 95 common dialogs, or some variation thereof. Your application should be fully compatible with short cuts, or link files. Be sure not to display the .3 extension of a file name in your application's title bar and that you follow the "Document Name - Application Name" naming convention. Use of the Windows 95 online help system should also be supported.

Windows NT compatibility...

This requirement is still around from the old Windows 3.1 logo program, although now the chances are much better that your software will run OK on NT. Because both Windows 95 and Windows NT are 32-bit and use the Win32 API, a properly written application should run happily on either platform. If you are using a feature that is specific to Windows 95 and is not available on NT, your software's functionality should "degrade gracefully," as Microsoft puts it.

Long filename support...

Besides hiding all .3 file name extensions, your product must also support long file names in order to be considered Windows 95-compatible. Supporting long file names takes a lot more than simply using the Windows 95 file Open and Save As dialogs. Your application must be able to use long file names in its title bars, dialogs, controls, and in the Windows 95 shell.

Plug and Play awareness...

You won't be denied the logo if you don't support Plug and Play. However, it is highly recommended that you do. Here are some reasons why supporting Plug and Play is a good idea:

- If the user inserts or removes a media device, chances are that you'll want to know about it.

- If the user changes the screen size, it would be nice if your windows automatically resized.

- If a computer's battery is running low, warning the user to save or shut down would be a nice gesture.

The next three requirements are only for document-based applications. By that I mean applications that have the ability to open and save documents via the File menu. It is important to distinguish a document-based application from a game or a utility that allows the user to simply save and retrieve settings using a File menu. These types of applications do not need to support OLE, UNC path names, and simple Send Mail.

OLE support (for document-based applications)...

In order to use the Windows 95-compatible logo, a document-based application must support OLE. This means that the application must either have the ability to contain OLE objects or provide objects that can be contained by other OLE applications. The user must be able to invoke the OLE features of your application using drag and drop. If your application is a container, the user should be able to drop an object into your document, or, if your application provides objects, the user should be able to drag them into another OLE application's document.

In addition, if your application is an OLE container, it should save files using the OLE structured storage compound file format. OLE compound files allow your application to save its data and the data of any embedded objects together in one file. The OLE compound file should support a Summary Information section as described in the Microsoft OLE 2.0 Reference manual.

(For more information on OLE, see the **Object Linking and Embedding** section earlier in this chapter.)

UNC path support (for document-based applications)...

To pass the Windows 95 compatibility test, document-based applications must support Universal Naming Convention (UNC) paths. UNC paths remove the need for drive letters. Instead, they allow you to access a network from any location using a simple path name. A UNC path name looks something like the following: *\\Server\Share\Directory\Filename.ext*. Because these can get quite long, you can see why it is essential to support long file names.

Send Mail support (for document-based applications)...

The last of the requirements, for document-based applications, is a simple mail-enabled File menu. Your application must provide the user with a "Send..." or "Send Mail..." command from the File menu. Adding a Send Mail command is simple, thanks to the Messaging API (MAPI) Software Development Kit (SDK) available from Microsoft. Windows 95 is suppose to allow your application to Send Mail without worrying about what email or network system is running in the background. Whether this is entirely true, I'm not so sure.

CHAPTER FOUR

How to Help

In the end, no matter how great your interface is, chances are that some users will not understand everything about your application. This is the hole that can be closed up by a well-designed help system. To what extent it fills the hole, like anything else, depends entirely on just how much time and effort you're willing to expend.

From a software developer's point of view, software is made up of three distinct elements: the installation program, the actual product, and the online help. These three components turn an ordinary program into a professional and marketable software product (provided that your idea was good enough from the beginning). Slapping together a quick and dirty online help file, or, worse yet, leaving one out altogether, could prove to be a bad mistake.

In the last chapter we focused on the guidelines that make or break a product's interface, and here we discuss online help and the standards that should be followed when designing it. In addition, this chapter introduces you to the elements that make up the Windows 95 help system. You're shown what's involved in implementing different types of user assistance—such as simple tool tips, "What's This?" help, and a Help Topics window. Keep one thing in mind, however: it really doesn't matter a whole lot how well you implement your online help if the help text is poorly written.

Designing Online Help

A Windows 95 application can assist the user in a variety of ways: by having a well-designed interface, including an easy to read manual, and by providing online help. Online help goes way beyond including a simple help file with your application. It is an integral part of software design, and, for this reason, appears here, in its own chapter.

Context-Sensitive Help

For help text to be considered *context-sensitive*, it must be displayed in context with the item it is attempting to clarify. In addition, the user must be able to request assistance directly from the item in question. This can be done either passively, as with tool tips, or actively, as with a Help button. In this section, we examine some of the various techniques you can use to incorporate context-sensitive help into your product's interface. Feel free to combine the different types of context-sensitive help in your product. When it comes to assisting the user, there's no such thing as too much redundancy.

Text in a Window

On its simplest level, context-sensitive help can be additional text that appears directly in a window. As long as it doesn't unduly clutter up the user's screen, a simple explanatory sentence or two is sometimes all it takes to clarify an issue. However, it is important to remember that too much text in a window can get to be annoying and disruptive to more experienced users.

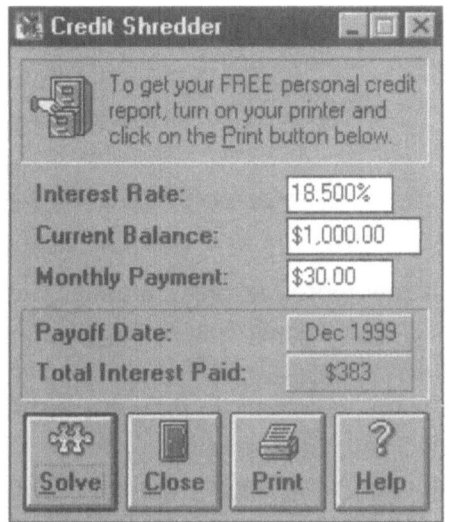

Sometimes a simple sentence is worth a thousand pictures.

If your screen real estate permits, text in a window may be the way to go when it comes to providing context-sensitive help. Placing your help text in its own panel, as in the example shown above, is some times an effective way to distinguish it from the other controls on a window. If you do decide to use text in a window, consider standardizing a particular look and feel. You can do this by using a catchy graphic (e.g., a light bulb or a question mark), or by changing the font attributes of the help text. This will help your users easily distinguish what is an on-screen tip from what is just regular text.

Status Bars and Tool Tips, Revisited

Status bars and tool tips are two types of context-sensitive help that often go hand in hand. In the previous chapter we talked a little bit about both of them when discussing the different types of controls available. Here we look at them with respect to how they can enhance your application's online help system.

Although a tool tip is just that, a few words at most, a status bar can accommodate a whole sentence. Use a status bar to display additional information about the current object—such as when the user presses the tab key to move from one object to the next, highlights a new menu item, or when a tool tip is displayed. Use tool tips to provide the user with a quick description of a control that does not already have a caption of its own (as with many toolbar buttons). You could, theoretically, make your tool tip text as long as a status bar message, but this is not recommended. Because of their nature, tool tips can really become annoying, and quite funny looking, when they display too much text.

"What's This?" Help

Another way that you can add context-sensitive help to your Windows 95 applications is by using "What's This?" style help. Unlike the prior two examples of context-sensitive help, "What's This?" help requires the user to play a more active role, rather than a passive one. With "What's This?" style help, the user decides when and for what object help text should be displayed. There are four different ways you can add "What's This?" style help to your product: make it a choice from the Help menu, create a toolbar button for it, use a secondary window's title bar to access it, or access it directly from an object's pop-up menu (via the right mouse button). Again, feel free to use one or all of these in your product.

Now, let's take a close look at each one.

From the Help menu...

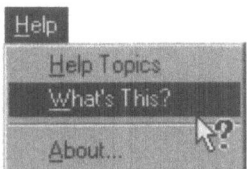

Having a "What's This?" menu command on your application's Help menu allows your users to actively request assistance. When a user first chooses the "What's This?" menu item from the Help menu, the mouse pointer switches from the default arrow to an arrow with a question mark (as in the picture shown above). From here, the user is able to point and click, using the mouse, on any object in the current window. This, in turn, causes pop-up help text to be displayed directly over the item in question (as in the picture shown below).

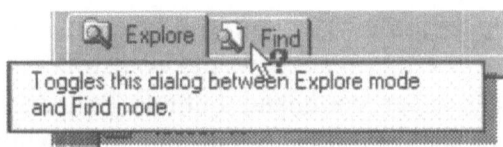

From a toolbar...

If your application's primary window has a toolbar, consider adding a "What's This?" toolbar button. This button should behave identically to the "What's This?" menu item. The button itself should be a two-state button. In other words, when the user clicks on this button it should remain pushed down until the user has clicked on an object with the arrow/question mark mouse pointer. At that point, pop-up help text can be displayed and the "What's This?" toolbar button can return to its original up state. Remember that, as with any toolbar button, there should always be a corresponding menu command that allows the user to do the same thing via the keyboard, instead of using the mouse.

Notice how the "What's This?" menu item works nicely in conjunction with a "What's This?" toolbar button. Although you don't have to use the two of them together, it is highly recommended that you do.

From a secondary window's title bar...

Because most secondary windows do not typically have a toolbar, or even a menu bar for that matter, there needs to be another way to provide the user with "What's This?" style help. Prior to Windows 95, the only way to do this was by having a "What's This?" command button alongside other command buttons. This worked just fine, except that this feature would sometimes get lost amongst a window's other command buttons (which, to make matters worse, often included a Help button). Now, thanks to Windows 95, you no longer have to use a command button in your secondary windows in order to provide "What's This?" style help. Instead, you can use a "What's This?" title bar button (shown in the above picture). The "What's This?" title bar button appears directly to the left of the window's close button and behaves just like the "What's This?" toolbar button (described under the previous topic).

From an object's pop-up menu...

The last way that you can incorporate "What's This?" style help into your Windows 95 software is via the right mouse button. When the user clicks the right mouse button on an object in Windows 95, a context-sensitive pop-up menu should be displayed. One of the items on this menu can be a "What's This?" help command. If there are no other menu items to include on a particular object's pop-up menu, it is OK to display just the "What's This?" command (as in the picture shown above).

The F1 Key

The F1 key is the oldest type of context-sensitive help there is. It's been floating around since the days of DOS, and is still an old favorite among many users. Ideally, your application should display context-sensitive help whenever the user presses the F1 key from anywhere in your program. Realistically, however, because the online help text will not cover everything, the F1 key should, at the very least, display the Help Topics window. This will allow the user to manually browse your online help and look for any applicable information. (For more on the Help Topics window see the upcoming section.)

From a user's point of view, the F1 key is probably the most efficient way to get online help. Similarly, the escape key should be the quickest way to close it. Not every online help file responds to the escape key, however. In order to enable this feature, the person writing the online help file must use a macro. We talk a little bit more about this later, in the "Creating Help Files" section of this chapter. Nevertheless, when it comes to designing your online help system, the F1 key and the escape key go hand in hand with one another, as do tool tips and status bars.

Using a Help Button

Help

Then there is always the Help button. From a software designer's point of view, using a Help button here and there has always been the easiest way to feel as if you're providing real context-sensitive help to your users. Be aware, however, that, even though it is, in a sense, a form of context-sensitive help, the help text that is displayed when a Help button is clicked is usually relevant to the entire window, not just to each of the individual objects on that window, as is the case with the other types of context-sensitive help. Also, keep in mind that both the Help button and the F1 key will typically open up a separate help window instead of simply displaying a pop-up help message that remains *in-context* with the item in question.

Help Topics

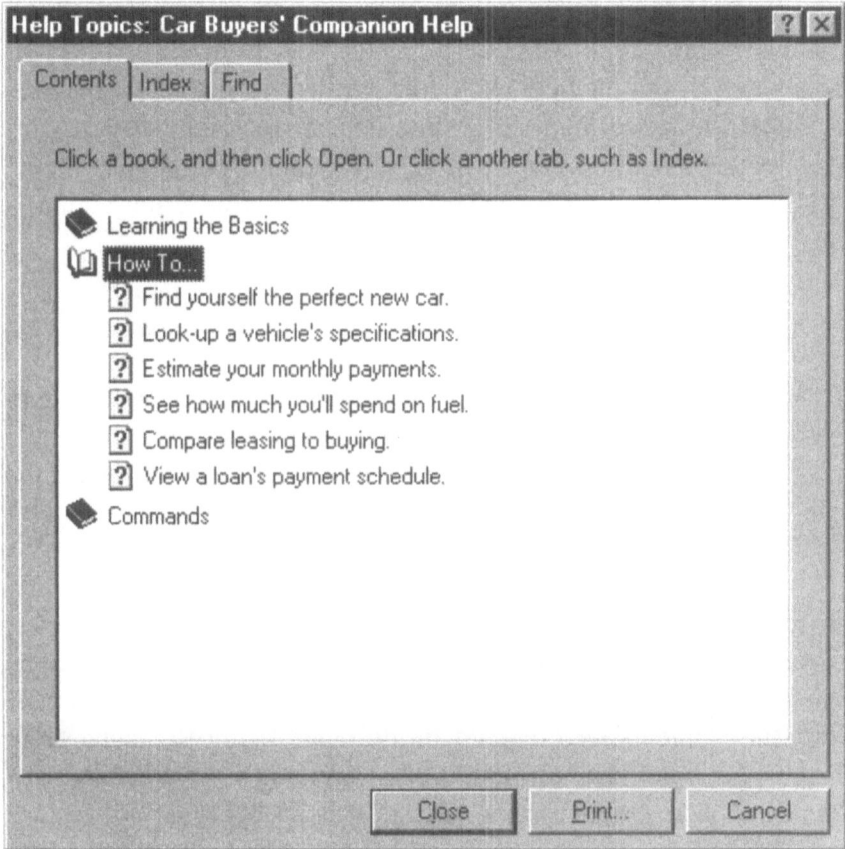

The biggest difference between designing online help for Windows 95 and Windows 3.1 is, without a doubt, the Help Topics window. The Help Topics window requires you to organize your online help in a hierarchical topics list. Because of this, you'll want to spend ample time thinking about the structure and layout of your help text. Also, you'll want to distinguish between what is instructional help and what is simply reference style documentation.

The Windows 95 Help Topics window should be the nerve center of a product's online help. This one simple window allows you to browse and navigate all of the help text using a table of contents, quickly locate a topic using an index, or find occurrences of a specific word within the help text using a powerful search engine. Because of the power and sheer simplicity of the Help Topics window, your product only needs to have two items on its Help menu, "Help Topics" and "What's This?" (provided you're not counting the "About..." box, of course).

Contents

Prior to Windows 95, adding a table of contents to your online help could only be done by using underlined jump text within a help file. With the introduction of the Help Topics window, you now can design your entire online help around this one, easy to use, window.

The Help Topics window is organized into three tabbed pages: Contents, Index, and Find. The Contents page uses a hierarchical list (a tree view control) to provide an online table of contents. Ideally, the Contents page should be designed using the same techniques that would be required to design a book's table of contents. In fact, if your product has a manual, it is probably not a bad idea to keep both it and the online help pretty much the same, hence eliminating the need to maintain two different sets of text.

(This is as good a time as any to digress a little bit with respect to the issue of online help versus paper documentation. Online help should not replace the need for a manual. Besides the fact that reading text on the screen causes too much eye strain, including a manual is sometimes all it takes to make your software feel like a real product and not just like another piece of shareware.)

Index

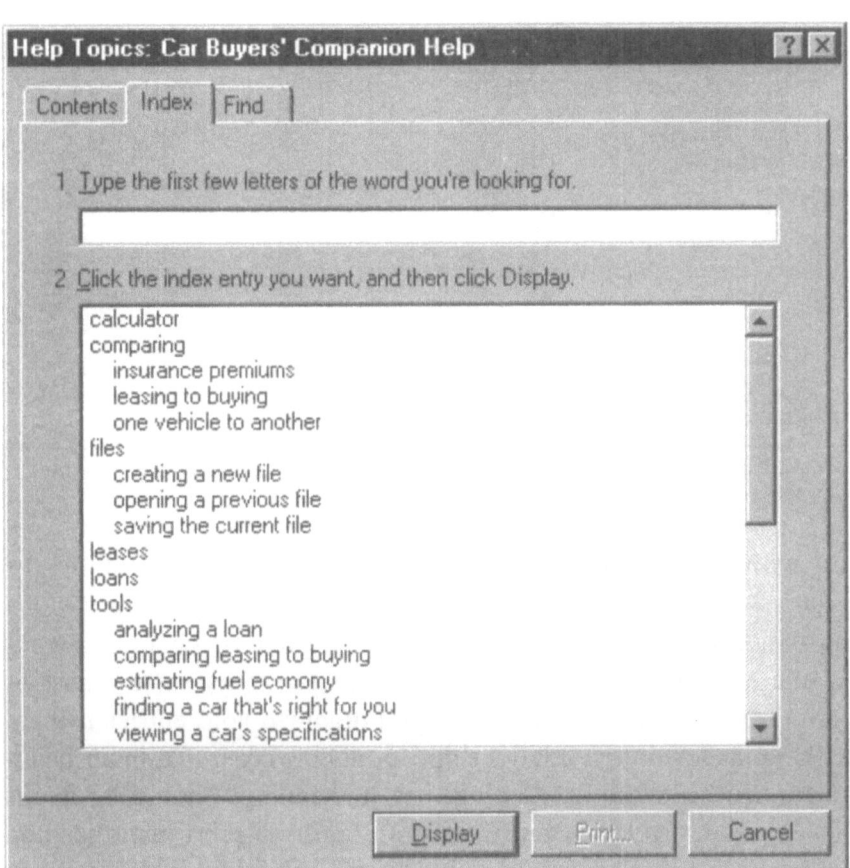

The second tab page of the Help Topics window displays an online help index. From the Index page, the user can either double-click on an index entry or use the Display button to open the help text for a specific item. If more than one related topic is found, the Topics Found dialog is displayed (see the following). This dialog allows the user to choose a topic from a list of related topics.

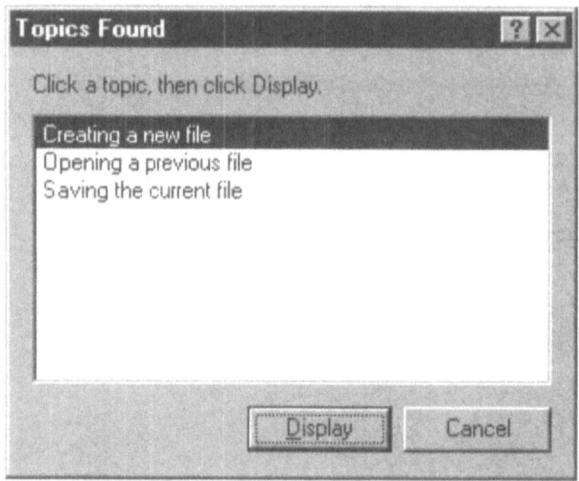

The Topics Found dialog allows the user to choose a topic from a list of"
related topics.

As with the Contents page, designing an online index requires the
same skills that go into creating a manual. Indexing is a discipline
in and of itself, so be extra careful when designing a help index. As
a rule of thumb, make sure that your index is not more than two
levels deep. Also, make sure that you organize your entries using a
consistent noun/verb relationship. In other words, if a main heading is a verb (such as opening), its subheadings should be nouns
(such as files, folders, and windows). Likewise, if a main heading
is a noun (such as files), its subheadings should be verbs (such as
opening, creating, and saving).

Find

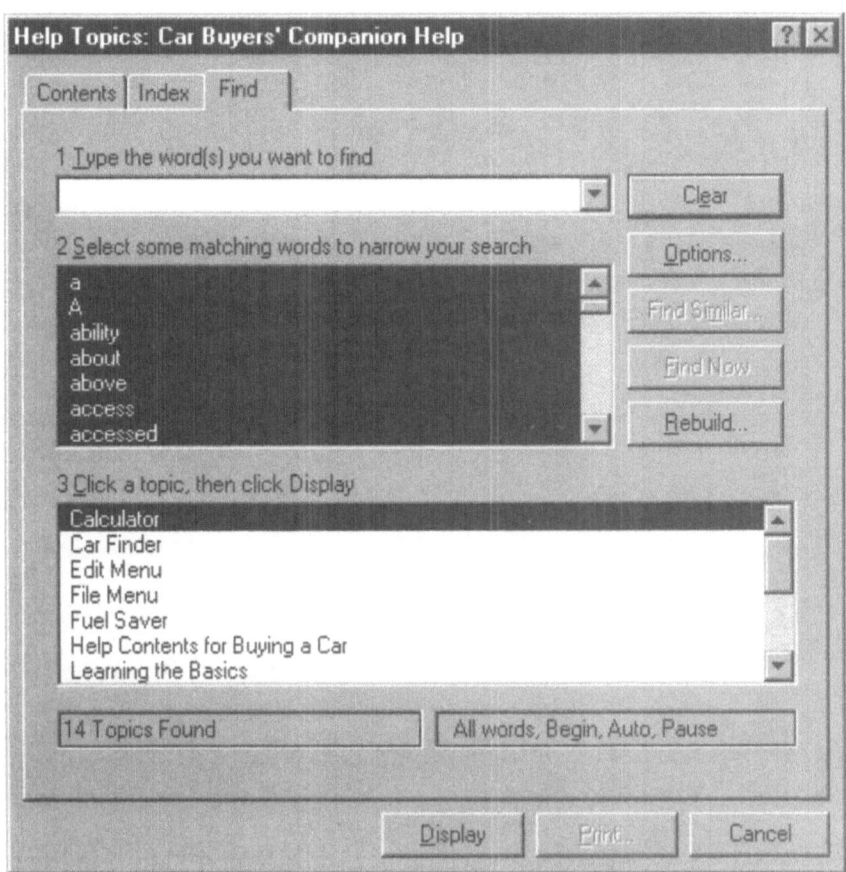

The Find page of the Help Topics window is definitely the easiest to implement. This is because Windows 95 handles everything for you. In order to provide the ability to search for individual words, Windows 95 must first create a small database. Clicking on the Find tab for the first time opens the "Find Setup Wizard" dialog (see the **Using Wizards** section of this chapter). This dialog gives the user three choices regarding the scope and size of the search database. Once the database has been created, however, the user will no longer have to go through this dialog. Instead, the Find page will automatically be displayed.

| Task Help |

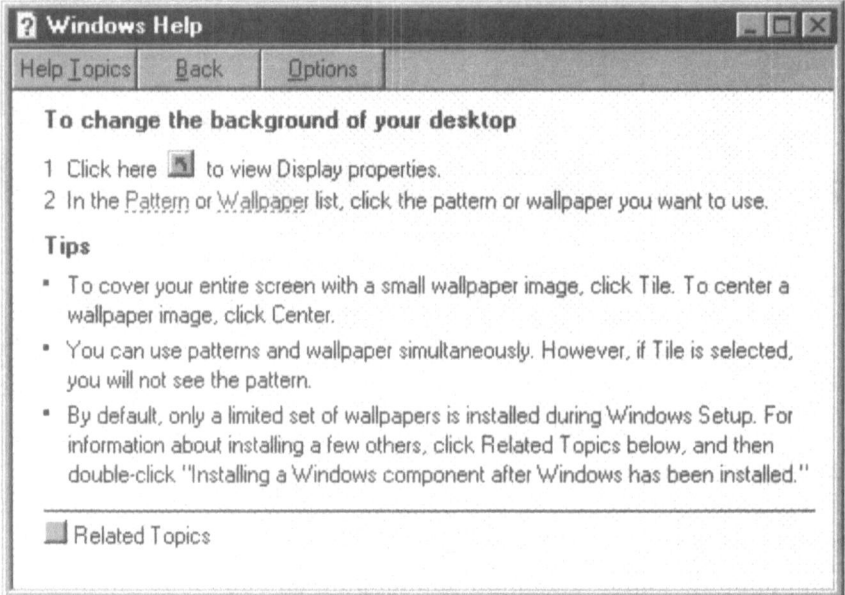

Along with the Help Topics window, task-oriented help windows are another significant change in the way online help should be designed. Using task-oriented help allows you to focus on instructional rather than informational text, and provides a standardized approach to designing *how to* style assistance.

Before Windows 95, if you recall, there weren't many guidelines to follow with respect to designing online help. In particular, there was no standardized way to distinguish between what was task-oriented help and what was simply online documentation. Because of this, in many cases, one or the other would often be left out altogether. Although some products' help text would explain how to do things in a step-by-step manner, others would be more like reading a book. When it comes to online help, some may argue that only the former is really necessary, but I disagree with that. I think a good mixture of both makes for an excellent online help system. You can do this by ensuring that the Contents page of your Help Topics window has one heading—which might be entitled "How To..."—for task help and other, more traditional, headings for reference help.

(For information on reference help, see the upcoming section.)

Writing Task Help

Use the following guidelines when writing text for task help windows:

📝 Overall, you should always try to keep your text conversational, yet concise. There is no need to be overly verbose. For example, a phrase such as, "To analyze your loan payments, click Calculate." is preferable to one that reads, "Clicking calculate will display your loan payments using the information you have entered."

📝 The first line of text should be bold and describe the task that is to be explained. For example, **"To scan a drive for viruses."** This text should closely resemble the topic that was chosen from the Help Topics window. The following lines of text should be enumerated and describe, step-by-step, how to carry out the action. Try not to use more than five steps, with each step being only one sentence in length.

✎ If you need to provide more information, consider adding a **Tips** section that contains a bulleted list of additional pointers.

Task Help Windows

Task help windows have a slightly different appearance from main (reference) help windows. Besides the lack of a menu bar, task help windows have a different background color. This color should be the same as a tool tip's background color (which is a system-defined color).

Let's now take a look at the specific items that, along with your text, can appear inside a task help window.

Button bar...

Every task help window should have a button bar that contains, at the very least, a Help Topics button, a Back button, and an Options button. The Help Topics button allows the user to quickly return to the Help Topics window at any point. Clicking on the Back button returns the user to the previous topic. This can be done repeatedly until the user is back to the original starting point. The Options button provides a way for the user to copy and print help text, and to change the appearance of the help window (e.g., font size and window position).

Shortcut buttons...

Along with your text, you can assist the user by including a shortcut button to help automate a certain task. Because the task help window is, by default, a topmost window that remains on top of other windows, you can help navigate the user to a particular spot. For example, step one may read something like, "1. Click here 🔲 to open the loan calculator." In this example, clicking on the shortcut button would automatically open the loan calculator window for the user. In the meantime, the user is still able to read the remaining steps from the task help window.

Typically, there is only one shortcut button per topic. This should make perfect sense if your task help is written correctly, because there should only be one task described in each topic.

Related topics...

Whenever there are more topics that relate to the current topic, a Related Topics button should appear as the last item in a task help window. Clicking on this button opens the topics found dialog. This allows the user to select a related topic from a list.

Jumps...

Think of jump text as "What's This?" help for your help. Jump text allows the user to display a pop-up window that further explains an item. Although task help jump text is typically green and underlined with a dotted line, in reality, there are two types of jump text you can use. Jump text that is underlined with a dotted line indicates that the jump simply displays a pop-up window. Jump text that is underlined with a solid line actually jumps you to a different topic. The user is then able to return to the previous topic by clicking on the Back button.

Reference Help

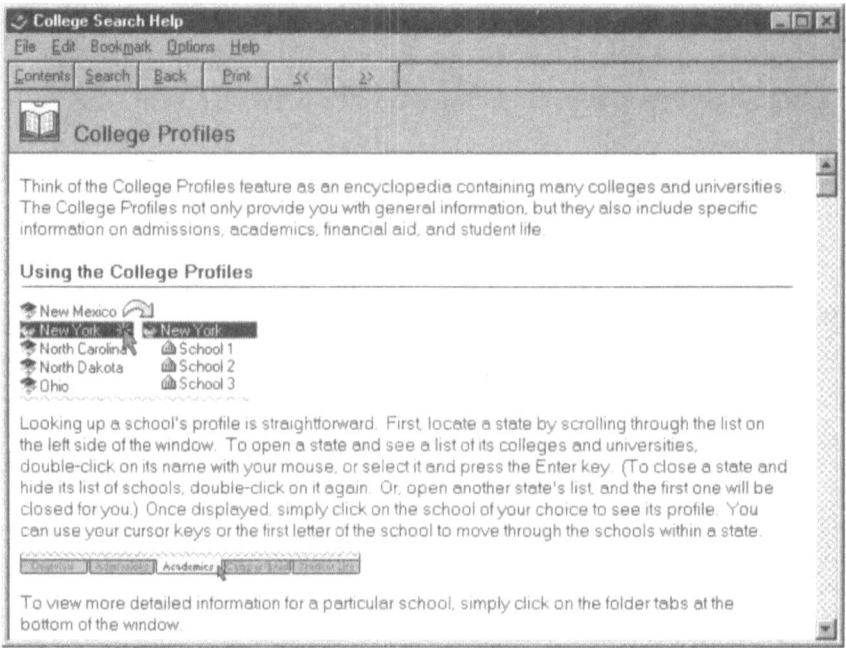

The other type of online help is sometimes called *reference help* and is displayed using a main help window (shown above). This is what most Windows 3.1 users would regard as online help. When it comes to lengthy discussions, online documentation, or a heavy use of graphics, video, and sound, reference help is far better suited than task help.

Writing Reference Help

If you're in a hurry, already have loads of help text written, or are porting to Windows 95, then reference help may be just the thing you need. Except for the fact that you can include jumps in your text, reference help is not too different from standard documentation. It can contain any mixture of text and graphics and be organized in any way you choose.

Reference help is usually designed around a contents topic. The contents topic displays a list of other topics contained in the help file. By clicking on this list of jumps, the user is able to visit the other topics in the help file. It is important not to confuse the contents topic of a help file (which is displayed in a main help window) with the Contents page of the Help Topics window. It is easy to see how this could happen. In Windows 3.1, using a contents topic was the only way to provide a table of contents for online help. Now, it is up to the Help Topics window to display the table of contents.

If you're only including reference help with your product, consider, at the very least, adding a Contents page to the Help Topics window. Because the Help Topics window can open both task help windows and reference help windows, you can still include a Contents page with your online help. This will allow your online help to look and feel like that of a true Windows 95 application with minimal effort. If your help text is well written, many users may not even notice the lack of task help.

(For more information on creating a contents file for the Help Topics window see the last part of this chapter.)

Main Help Windows

A main help window is a primary window that is used to display reference style help text. It has a menu bar, a button bar, and the ability to open secondary windows. Main help windows have a different look and feel than task help windows. When first displayed, main help windows are typically larger in dimension than task help windows, and are often centered on the screen as opposed to being off to one side (task help windows usually appear to the right of the screen). Also, main help windows typically have just a plain white background, unlike task help windows, which have the same background color as that of the tool tips.

As well as displaying text in a scrolling region, a main help window provides a variety of other features that enhance a product's online reference help. Let's take a look at some of these.

Menu bar...

File   Edit   Bookmark   Options   Help

Unlike task help windows, main help windows have a menu bar. By default, the menu bar allows the user to open a different help file, print the current help topic, copy help text to the clipboard, attach a note to a help topic, define multiple bookmarks, and display a copyright message. Can you believe it? All that functionality without doing a thing! In addition, the Options menu allows the user to control the visual aspects of a main help window, just as the Options button does on a task help window.

If that's not enough for you, however, you can still use macros to customize your main help window's menu bar. Macros allow you to customize the menu bar by inserting new menus, appending menu items to existing menus, and by controlling the appearance and behavior of those items. We talk a little bit more about macros later in this chapter.

Button bar...

If you recall, every task help window should have certain buttons on its button bar (Help Topics, Back, and Options). In this sense, the button bar on a main help window is no different. At the very least, it should have a Contents, a Search, a Back, and a Print button. The Contents button allows the user to quickly return to either the Help Topics table of contents or the help file's contents topic. If a help file (.hlp) has a corresponding contents file (.cnt), then, when the user clicks on the Contents button, the Help Topics window will open with the contents page selected. Otherwise, the help file's contents topic is displayed. The Search button displays the Help Topics window with the Index page activated. From here, the user is able to search the index for a particular word. The Back button is used to cycle back through a history of all previously visited topics. And the Print button does just that—prints the current topic.

In addition, many products also include an Index button and/or browse buttons (shown in the picture above). The Index button is used to open a secondary window from which the user can click on an alphabetized index entry. Browse buttons (<</>>) allow the user to move sequentially, back and forth, through a series of related pages.

Just as the menu bar, the button bar can also be customized. In addition to choosing from a list of predefined buttons (such as the browse buttons), you can also define your own buttons using macros. The Index button is an example of a custom button.

Nonscrolling regions...

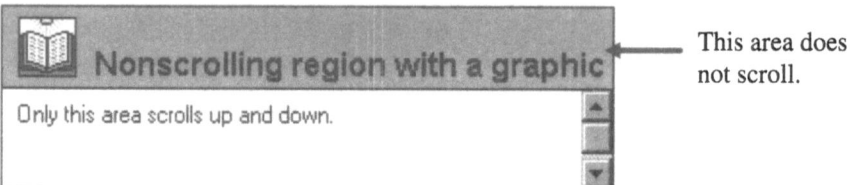

This area does not scroll.

The primary function of any help window is to display help text. In order to accommodate a limited amount of screen space, the help text is, more often than not, displayed in a scrollable region. You can create a nonscrolling region that is always visible regardless of where the scroll bar is positioned. Doing this can make your online help look very savvy and polished. The nonscrolling region is a great place to display the name of the current topic using a nice bold font. You can also include graphics here as well.

Jumps...

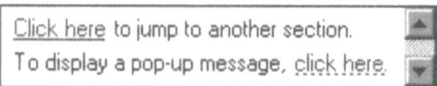

Jumps are really what sets apart online help from traditional documentation. It's the ability for the user to quickly jump to a related topic while reading another that makes hypertext such a powerful feature. All the while, the user need not worry about getting lost, thanks to the Back button.

As was said earlier, clicking on text that is underlined with a dotted line (as in the example shown above) will display a pop-up window instead of jumping to another topic (as would a word that is underlined with a solid line).

Graphics...

In many cases, a picture is worth a thousand words, so making good use of them in your online help is essential. Online help supports a variety of different picture formats, such as bitmaps, hotspot graphics, and multiple resolution bitmaps.

Hotspot graphics allow multiple clickable regions to be designated on a single bitmap. For example, you may want to include an image of a map of the United States that allows the user to click on individual states. This can be done quite easily using the hotspot editor.

To ensure that your graphics will always appear to be the same size regardless of the user's particular hardware setup, consider using multiple resolution bitmaps. Multiple resolution bitmaps will handle differences in aspect ratios and video resolutions by allowing Windows help to automatically distort them. The only drawbacks are that you will have to compile your bitmaps using the multiple resolution bitmap compiler and that, unfortunately, they do not compress as well as regular bitmaps.

Secondary Help Windows

First, to avoid confusion, let's recap a bit. Not counting context-sensitive help, there are two fundamental types of online help available in Windows 95: task help and reference help. Task help deals with task-oriented, or procedural, assistance and is displayed using the smaller task help windows. Reference help deals with documentation style help and is displayed using a main help window, which can, in turn, display secondary help windows. Both task help and reference help can be opened from the Help Topics window. Got that?

Now let's talk a little bit about secondary help windows, using an Index button as an example. If the user clicks on a main help window's Index button (assuming it has one), chances are that a secondary help window will be opened. Secondary help windows can have all the characteristics of a main help window, but will, more often than not, lack a menu bar. Secondary help windows should not be confused with task help windows, which—though they don't have a menu bar either—have a different look and feel altogether.

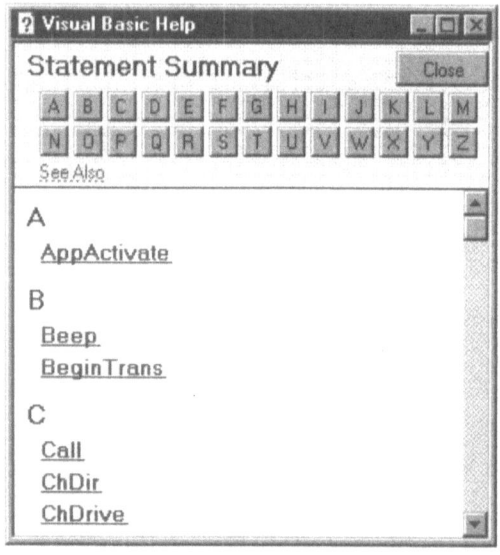

Microsoft Visual Basic uses a secondary help window to display an index."

Wizards

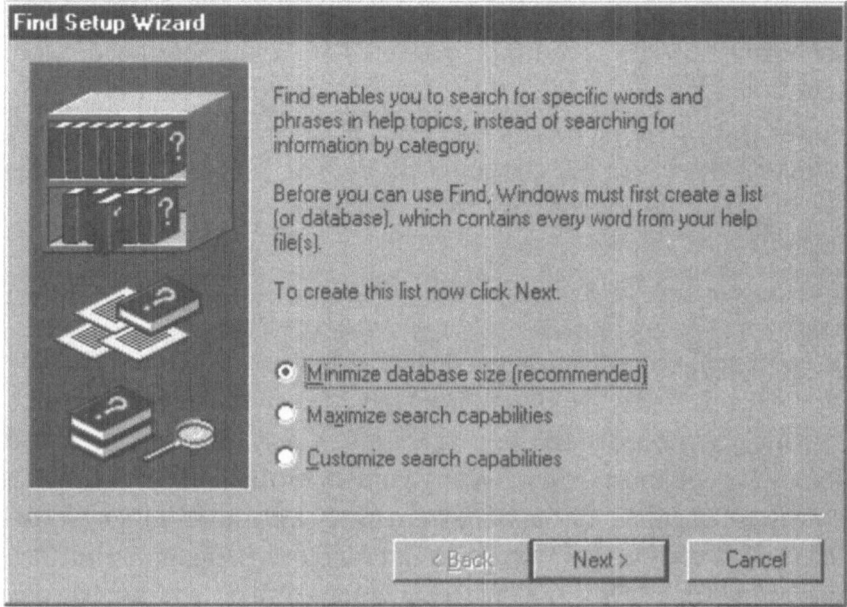

The Help Topics' Find tab uses a wizard to create a small database of" words.

Another way to provide user assistance is by using wizards. Wizards can help simplify what would otherwise be an overly complex process. The concept behind wizards is to help guide the user, step-by-step, in a hand-holding manner. To do this effectively, wizards should always be conversational, friendly, and forgiving. Think of them as an agent acting between the user and the software.

Although wizards do serve a useful purpose, they also have a couple of pitfalls of which you should be aware. Oftentimes, wizards can be used to an extreme. By attempting to clarify what is already rather easy, simplicity is sometimes sacrificed and the user's intelligence may be insulted. For these reasons, wherever there is a wizard, there should also be a more traditional way of accomplishing the same thing. Even though displaying information in a sequential manner is easier to comprehend, it can not compare with the efficiency and speed that is offered by a well-designed, more traditional interface. Also, the wizard interface is technically more complicated to implement from both a designer's and a developer's point of view. Think about it, instead of creating one simple screen, multiple screens have to be designed.

Writing Wizard Text

If you recall from the context-sensitive help section, you'll notice that wizards make use of another type of user assistance: text in a window. Writing wizard text is an art in and of itself. First and foremost, you must define writing guidelines that will be used, in a consistent manner, throughout the entire wizard. In other words, does each screen begin with an introductory paragraph and then pose a question? Or is the question displayed first, in bold text, say, and then additional text follows? You get the idea. It is important to establish these guidelines ahead of time in order to maintain a consistent look and feel.

After you've established your guidelines, you can begin writing text for your wizard's pages. Try to use the following pointers as you do that:

🖉 Each wizard page should try to focus on only one logical thing at a time. That doesn't mean you can't have the user do more than one thing on each page. For example, a mailing address requires filling in multiple fields. It would be silly to prompt the user for each field using separate wizard pages.

🖊 Try to keep the total number of pages (per wizard) relatively low.

🖊 Do not use technical jargon. This defeats the purpose of using a wizard altogether.

🖊 Wizard text should be written in a conversational, yet clear and concise, manner.

🖊 Don't be afraid to address the user directly, using words such as, "you" and "your."

🖊 Use the present tense. For example, instead of saying "Clicking Next will create this list." say "To create this list, click Next.'"

🖊 Always ask the users what to do, instead of telling them what to do. This makes them feel as if they are in control. Keep in mind, just because a sentence ends with a question mark doesn't mean it sounds like a question. For example, text such as "How do you want to sort this list?" is far better than something like "Sort this list using which order?"

Wizard Windows

You've heard the old saying, "You can spot a wizard a mile away." Well, maybe not, but that does ring kind of true. Unfortunately, wizard windows aren't just another type of window from which you can simply choose. Quite to the contrary, it is up to you to ensure that your wizards look and feel the way a wizard should.

Three things make a wizard a wizard: the writing style of the text (which was just discussed), the overall layout of the window, and a set of navigational buttons. Here are the guidelines you should follow for the latter two:

Layout...

If you take a look at the wizard that is displayed back on page 115, you'll be able to see the basic layout of a wizard window. Typically, this is the look most wizards have. Although no one is forcing you to use this look, users have come to expect it.

When it comes to wizard windows, it is not uncommon for the title bar to have the word "wizard" in it. For example, if you're creating a wizard that helps the user find the car of his dreams, you could call it the "Car Finder Wizard".

In terms of actual layout, the left side of a wizard window is typically used to display a catchy graphic. This graphic should relate to either the current page or the entire wizard as a whole. The right side of a wizard window is, without a doubt, where the meat and potatoes go. This part can be further broken down into a top half and a lower half. The top half is used to display the wizard text. The bottom half is where the user replies. The very bottom of a wizard window should be reserved for command buttons—this includes the navigational buttons discussed in the following. In addition, a divider line is often used to visually set the button area apart from the rest of the window.

Wizard buttons...

The navigational buttons that appear along the bottom of a wizard window are what makes the wizard interface possible. The wizard command button set includes a Back, a Next, and a Cancel button. The Cancel button should change to a Finish button once the user has reached the last page of the wizard. Similarly, the Back button should be disabled while on the first page, as should the Next button while on the last page.

Notice how the Back and the Next button use the less than (<) and the greater than characters (>). These two characters have come to be the international symbols for backward and forward. If you want to provide a button that allows the user to quickly return to the first page of a wizard, consider adding something like a "<< First" button. In this case, the double "<<" visually signifies a bigger change.

Creating Online Help

Even if you're not the person responsible for writing online help, having a thorough understanding of how it works can only benefit your ability to design it. This section is by no means intended to be a quick tutorial that will have you writing help files in a jiffy. Instead, it focuses on the underlying framework of the Windows 95 help environment. The more you understand it, the more capable you will be with respect to designing great online help.

Now that we've talked a whole lot about the aspects of designing online help, let's take a closer look behind the scenes, at what's involved in creating it.

Overview

As was said before, back in Chapter Two, how can you really know what is possible, in terms of interface design, unless you have a thorough understanding of the tools that go into making the product? Designing online help is no different in this respect. With all the improvements to Windows 95 help—most of which we've just discussed—it should come as no surprise that the process of creating it has not gotten any easier.

In order to incorporate online help into your application, a variety of files must first be in place. The help text itself must be contained in one or more files that have been saved as rich-text format (.rtf). RTF files are interchangeable text files that use embedded formatting information to display text and encoded bitmaps to display graphics. Just about every popular word processor supports this type of file format. The rich-text format enables most of the formatting features of a word processor to be applied directly to your help text. Because of this, having good page layout skills is of utmost importance when it comes to making your help text look nice. In addition to simply containing formatted help text and graphics, an RTF help file also makes extensive use of footnotes. Footnotes allow each page in an RTF file to be designated as a separate help topic. Footnotes serve other purposes as well, such as providing a place for index keywords.

Once your help text has been written, a help project file (.hpj) must be created. You can create a help project file using either a text editor (such as Notepad) or, preferably, the Microsoft Help Workshop (discussed in the following section). Among other things, the help project file contains a list of all the RTF files that make up your online help. (For more on help project files, see page 126.)

After the help project file has been created, it can be compiled within the Microsoft Help Workshop. Compiling a help project file creates a corresponding Windows help file (.hlp). This file can then be opened either manually, using the Windows help browser (WinHelp), or programmatically, from within your application.

The last file that needs to be in place before online help can be incorporated into your application is a contents file (.cnt) for the Help Topics window. Creating a contents file is a separate task altogether, but still requires the use of the Microsoft Help Workshop. Even though the contents file is the last step in the build process, it should be one of the first steps in the design process. If you recall from earlier in this chapter, the contents page of the Help Topics window is, for all intents and purposes, an online table of contents. Hence, designing it up front, regardless of the fact that you can't hook up any topics until the help file is complete, is definitely the way to go.

Rich-Text Format Files

Assuming you've read the last few paragraphs, you already have an idea of what rich-text format files are. Here we examine them in more detail in terms of how they are used to contain individual help topics. As far as online help is concerned, that's all an RTF file is, nothing more than a collection of help topics. Think of help topics as separate pages of varying length. Each individual help topic can range in size anywhere from a few simple words (as with "What's This?" pop-ups) to hundreds of words and pictures (as with reference help).

(If you can't stand the thought of using RTF files, go ahead and jump to the last part of this chapter **Help Authoring Systems**. Get it?)

Footnotes

Footnotes are the mechanism the RTF file uses to give the help compiler information about individual topics. At the beginning of each page (or topic) in an RTF file there can be a series of footnote symbols displayed. These symbols are again reflected in the foot-notes section of the page. How an individual word processor han-dles footnotes may differ slightly from one program to the next. Nevertheless, a footnote is a footnote.

The following table demonstrates the most common types of footnotes recognized by the Windows help compiler...

Symbol	Name	Description
#	Topic ID	Used to uniquely identify each topic. This footnote is the only one that is mandatory for each topic. The "IDH_" prefix should be used for all topics that are called from a program.
$	Title	Gives the topic a title. This title is displayed in other help windows (i.e., Topics Found, Bookmark, and History windows).
K	Keyword	The K footnote is used to link related keywords and/or topics to this topic. It is from this footnote that the Index page of the Help Topics window is built. Multiple entries are separated with a semicolon.
+	Browse Position	Specifies the position of this topic in a browse sequence.
!	Macro	Runs the specified macro when the topic is opened.
*	Build Tag	Used for conditional compilation. This allows you to keep a master topics list even though not every topic may be included in a particular build.
>	Window Type	Determines the type of window that should be used to display this topic. The different types of windows must be listed in the help project file.

Nonscrolling Regions

If you remember, back on page 112 you were introduced to nonscrolling regions. Adding them to your help file is a breeze. Simply select the first few lines of a topic's page, and then, using your word processor's paragraph formatting screen, mark them using the "Keep with next" option. That's all there is to it!

Jumps

If you thought adding a nonscrolling region was easy, wait until you see how simple it is to add a jump. First select the text you want to indicate as a jump. Then, underline it (using a double-line for a jump or a dotted line if you want a pop-up) and, directly to the right of it, insert the name of the topic ID you want to open when the user clicks on the jump text. Finally, select the topic ID you entered and, using your font formatting screen, designate it as hidden text. Not bad, huh?

Macros

The ability to use macros is what makes the Windows help environment so extendible. Macros allow you to customize the basic functionality of the help system in a programmatic way. There are seven basic types of macros you can use: button macros, menu macros, window macros, keyboard macros, program macros, link macros, and bookmark macros. Got that?

- Button macros allow you to create new buttons on the button bar and/or modify the functionality of existing buttons.

- Menu macros allow you to add new menus and/or modify existing ones.

- Window macros enable you to close other help windows, position them in a particular area, and/or modify their visual characteristics.

- Keyboard macros are used to trigger other macros whenever the user enters a certain keystroke.

- Program macros provide a way to launch other applications directly from help.

- Link macros are used to jump to other topics, either directly or indirectly, via the Topics Found dialog.

- And, finally, bookmark macros allow you to create, jump to, and test for bookmarks.

These macros can be used individually or can be combined with one another to provide greater functionality. For example, you may want to add a button to the button bar (using a button macro) that jumps to a particular topic when clicked (using a link macro). Or perhaps you want to allow the user to quickly close a help window whenever the escape key is pressed. This can be done using both a keyboard macro and a window macro.

Macros can be called from a variety of places, including other macros, as just shown in the prior two examples. If you want a macro to run every time a help file is opened, you can add a macro directly to the help project file. Macros can also be placed in topic footnotes—using the exclamation point "!" footnote symbol. Adding a macro to a footnote causes it to be run every time the topic is opened.

Microsoft Help Workshop

The Microsoft Help Workshop is a huge improvement over the Windows 3.1 help compiler (which actually ran under DOS). Thanks to this handy developer's tool, you can now create (notice I didn't say "write"), compile, and test your online help all within one application. It also allows you to create a contents file for the new Help Topics window using an easy to use visual environment. Besides an integrated RTF editor, what else could you ask for?

Help Project

The help project file can contain as many as eight different sections, all of which are represented by buttons on the project window (shown above). Instead of having to manually type in each section, as we did back in Windows 3.1, the Microsoft Help Workshop automates much of this work for us. Here's a brief description of each section.

- The Options section is used to set various project-specific items, such as the copyright, the title of the main help window, the default topic, and the level of compression, to name a few.

- The Files section is a list of all the RTF files that are included in the help file.

- The Windows section allows you to define custom window styles. These styles can include task help windows, main help windows, and secondary help windows. Once you've defined a window style, you can use it to display a topic (see page 123).

- If you're using bitmaps, you can either embed them directly in an RTF file or store them as separate bitmap files. If you choose the latter method, the Bitmaps section of the help project file allows you to specify the location of those files.

- The Map section frees you from having to keep track of numeric topic IDs by allowing you to assign them readable names. (Numeric IDs are necessary if you want to open a help file to a particular topic, as is the case with context-sensitive help.)

- The Alias section is just that; it allows you to equate one topic ID with another.

- The Config section is used to define startup macros. The macros that are listed here will run every time the help file is opened (see page 125).

- Because the help system's macro language can be extended (using a DLL), a Data Files section is sometimes necessary in order to keep track of any related files.

Help Contents

Creating a contents file for the Help Topics window is a cinch. If you recall, the contents page of the Help Topics window is nothing more than a separate file (.cnt) that contains a hierarchical list of help topics. Whenever a help file is opened, the Help Topics window will be displayed if there is a corresponding contents file. The contents file typically has the same name as the help file. However, a different name can be used if it is specified in the options section of the help project file. Back on page 100 we discussed the contents page from a design point of view; here we examine what's involved in creating one.

The Microsoft Help Workshop allows you to create a contents file in much the same way you would create a hierarchical menu using one of today's software development tools. Just about every menu editor out there offers a similar mechanism for inserting, deleting, indenting, and moving around menu items. The Help Workshop's

Edit, Remove, Add Above, Add Below, Move Right, and Move Left buttons (shown in the preceding picture) allow the user to design a contents page with the same facility as designing a menu.

Each time you create a new topic, using one of the Add buttons, you must also specify a topic ID and the name of the help file in which the topic resides. In addition, you can also designate the style of the window that should be used when the topic is displayed—assuming you've defined one in the help project file. A heading, on the other hand, only requires a title because it only displays a list of topics and/or subheadings. In the picture below, notice how you can also call a macro directly from the Help Topics window.

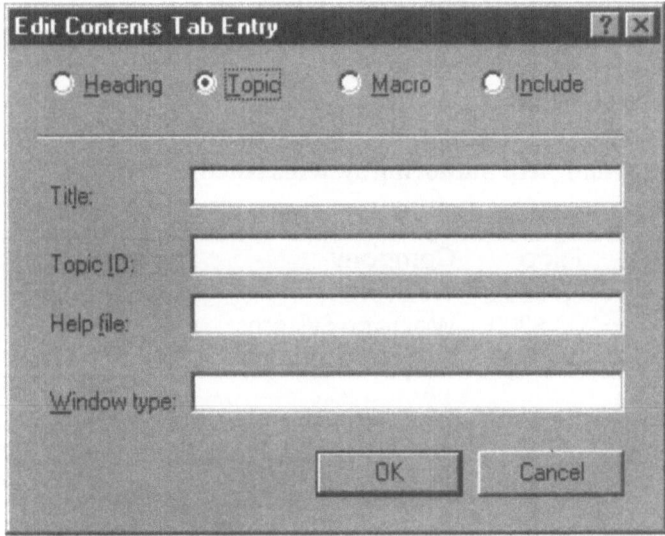

The Microsoft Help Workshop allows the user to enter items for the Help Topic's contents page using this dialog.

Help Authoring Systems

If you can't stand the technical heat, then you're in luck, my friend. There's a plethora of what are sometimes called, "help authoring systems" on the market. These integrated environments allow you to write your help text without ever once touching a footnote. How does that sound? The basic concept behind these systems is to shield you, as much as possible, from the complexity that goes on behind the scenes, hence letting you concentrate more on your writing than on your topic footnotes. It is important to keep one thing in mind, however: there is nothing they can do that can't be done without them. In other words, taking a little bit of extra time to learn the ins and outs of RTF files and how to use the Microsoft Help Workshop may be your best route, particularly if you're on a budget, or if you're planning a rather small help system.

Here are some popular help authoring systems listed in order of price...

Product	Price	Company	Phone
Visual Help Pro	$100-$200	WinWare	(800) 507-4357
Doc-To-Help	$200-$300	WexTech Systems	(800) 939-8324
RoboHELP	$400-$500	Blue Sky Software	(800) 571-9767

Connecting Online Help

So now that you've designed and created your help files, what do you do with them? How do you get your application to work with them? The answer to these questions depends on the development system you're using. While some development systems provide a simple way to integrate online help, others rely on a more programmatic approach. Let's take a look at some of the ways in which an application can be connected to a help file.

Using the API

Just about every Windows software development environment has access to the Windows API (Application Programming Interface). The Windows API is a collection of low-level routines that allow a program to function within the Windows environment. The modern day programmer is somewhat shielded from these low-level routines. For example, when a Visual Basic programmer wants to open a window, he simply uses a form's Show method. Behind the scenes, however, Visual Basic still needs to make the appropriate API calls required for opening a window. Similarly, a C++ programmer may be using a class library that in turn calls the API. This adds an extra layer of simplicity on top of the API. Nevertheless, using the API is, in many cases, the best way to get the job done.

When it comes to interacting with help files, the Windows API call, "WinHelp," is rather simple to implement. WinHelp requires four pieces of information from the programmer: the handle (ID) of the window that is requesting help, the directory-pathname of a help file, the type of help that is being requested (e.g., display a topic, display the contents page, display a pop-up), and any additional information that is required to complete the call (e.g., the topic ID). That's pretty much it! By just using this one API call, your application is able to fully interact with help files.

With Visual Basic

In addition to supporting the WinHelp API call, many development tools, such as Microsoft Visual Basic, provide even easier ways to connect an application to a help file. For example, a Visual Basic application can designate a global help file. For this reason, just about every control has a HelpContextID property and a WhatsThisHelpID property. When the user presses the F1 key, Visual Basic automatically opens the global help file and, if the current control has a help ID, the appropriate help topic is displayed.

Another way that Visual Basic can communicate with help files is via the common dialogs custom control. By simply setting a couple of properties (HelpFile and HelpCommand) and invoking the ShowHelp method, a Visual Basic application is connected to online help.

(For more information on Microsoft Visual Basic, see the upcoming chapter.)

CHAPTER FIVE

Prototyping 101

A prototype is the culmination of design. It represents an idea yearning to become reality. The better you can visualize your ideas, the more certain you will be about the choices you make. This is what helps bring us so close to perfection.

You can't really have a practical guide to Windows 95 interface design without a chapter on prototyping. After all, the prototype represents everything we worked for—oftentimes more so than the actual product. And, unless you know how to create one, you really can't convey your interface ideas very effectively.

In this chapter, you are introduced to the most popular prototyping tool in the industry, Microsoft Visual Basic. By no means does this imply that Visual Basic cannot be used to create a real application—quite the contrary. Visual Basic is, in my opinion, the most productive and efficient software development tool on the market. Nevertheless, with respect to this book, we look at it only from a prototyping point of view, as it is quite commonly used by many software companies.

(My obvious bias towards Visual Basic comes from my direct experiences with it. Over the course of two years, I was able to develop a total of six retail software products using it. Two were licensed to Parsons Technology and four related ones were sold to Kaplan Educational Centers.)

Introduction to Microsoft Visual Basic

Trying to teach you Visual Basic within the scope of one chapter is an impossible task. So instead, just as the heading reads, you'll be introduced to it in a way that will allow you to have a basic understanding of how it can be used to create a prototype.

(Because this book deals with designing software for Windows 95, we use the latest 32-bit version of Visual Basic 4.0 throughout this chapter.)

Overview

The Visual Basic environment works in two different modes: *design time* and *run time*. It is during *design time* that you actually build your prototype (or application) and spend most of your time. *Run time*, on the other hand, is when you're testing your prototype and using it in the same way a user would if she ran it directly from the Windows 95 shell.

Design time usually goes something like this:

1. You begin by creating a new project, which, by default, automatically creates a new form. (Visual Basic refers to windows as forms.)

2. You then place controls on your form.

3. Next, you customize the controls by setting their properties. (Properties define the characteristics of each control.)

4. And, finally, you write code. (This is the tricky part.) For example, you may want to fill a list box with some data, or open another window when the user clicks on a certain button.

5. You can then create additional forms and repeat steps 2, 3, and 4 for each new window.

Event-Driven Programming

Visual Basic is said to be an event-driven, object-based programming language. In other words, a Visual Basic application is made up of a collection of objects, each of which responds to certain events. Objects can be controls, forms, or classes. (You need not concern yourself with the latter. Classes are not necessary for creating prototypes.) Events can be triggered either directly (such as when the user clicks a mouse button or presses a key) or indirectly (from code you've written).

Even though most objects respond to their own unique set of events, there are some common events to which almost all objects respond. These more common events are the ones that are typically used in a prototype.

Just about every visible control responds to the following events...

Event name	Occurs if:
Click	A mouse button is clicked on an object.
DragDrop	A draggable object is dropped on an object.
DragOver	A draggable object is dragged over an object.
GotFocus	The user tabs onto an object, giving it the focus.
KeyDown	A keyboard key is pushed down.
KeyPress	A keyboard key is pushed down and released.
KeyUp	A keyboard key is released.
LostFocus	The user tabs off one object and onto another.
MouseDown	A mouse button is clicked on an object.

MouseMove	The mouse cursor is moved over an object.
MouseUp	A mouse button is released while over an object.

Notice how some of those events are compound events—made up of other smaller events. The Click event, for example, is made up of both a MouseDown and a MouseUp event. Likewise, the KeyPress event is made up of a KeyDown event and a KeyUp event.

In addition to properties and events, an object can also provide methods. Methods are a way an object allows you to control it from within your code. In other words, you use an object's methods to get it to do something. For example, a list box has an AddItem and a RemoveItem method. Just as you'd expect, these two methods allow you to add and remove items to and from a list box.

Windows

The Visual Basic integrated development environment consists of one primary window (the main toolbar) and a variety of secondary windows: a project window, the toolbox, and the properties window. In addition, you can use the project window to open forms and/or code windows. All of these are discussed in the following.

Main Toolbar

The main toolbar window is the nerve center of Visual Basic. In addition to providing quick and easy access to the most commonly used features in Visual Basic (via buttons), it also contains a menu bar. The File menu allows you to create a new project, save the current project, or open an existing project. You can also use the File menu to create a standalone executable of your prototype— that is, once you've finished it, of course. Just as you'd imagine, the Edit menu allows you to cut, copy, and paste items, such as controls on a form, or code in a code window. The View menu allows you to access the secondary windows (discussed in the following). And, the Insert menu allows you to add new forms to your project.

Up until now, all the menus discussed are used during *design time*. The Run menu, on the other hand, invokes and supports the *run time* features of Visual Basic. It allows you to try out your prototype, in much the same way a user would, and to debug it if need be.

Apart from the Help menu (which is just that), the remaining two menus (Tools and Add-Ins) are used to extend the functionality of Visual Basic. Although the Tools menu is primarily used to add custom controls to the current project, the Add-Ins menu is used to enhance the development environment itself.

Project Window

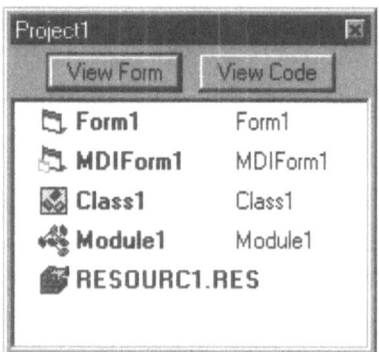

The Project window displays a list of all the files in your project. This list can include forms, an MDI form, classes, modules, and one resource file. You already know that a form is a window, so it should come as no surprise that an MDI form is an MDI parent window. And, because we're only dealing with prototypes, you can ignore classes and resource files altogether.

Modules, on the other hand, can come in quite handy when dealing with prototypes. Whenever there is some generic code that appears in more than one form, it is time to create a module. Modules are public collections of commonly used subroutines and functions.

From the Project window, you can open forms and/or code windows. Although every form has a corresponding code window, not every code window has a corresponding form window.

Toolbox

Once you've got a form displayed, you can go ahead and begin designing your interface. The Toolbox is a repository of all available controls in the current project. You can select a control to add to the current form by simply double-clicking on it from the Toolbox. Then you use your mouse to position it on the form and resize it. This is how you paint your interface.

Visual Basic comes with about 20 standard controls. If you have the Professional or the Enterprise edition, you'll also be able to add a variety of other controls to the Toolbox. Adding new controls is a snap. Simply select "Custom Controls..." from the Tools menu, and bingo! A list of all available controls will be displayed. From here, you can select the ones you want to use. Among these will be the Windows 95 common controls (i.e., list view, tree view, tabs, toolbar, status bar, slider, and progress indicator). You won't want to miss out on those, especially if you're designing software for Windows 95. (Which I assume is the main reason you're reading this book.)

Properties Window

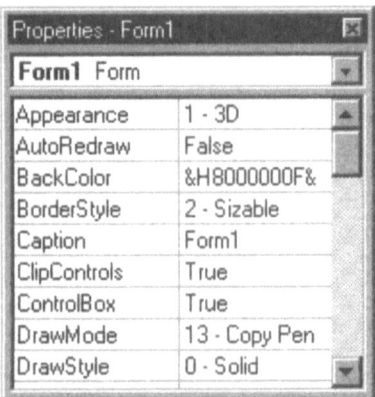

As you plop new controls down on a form, you'll quickly notice that they look rather generic. For example, command buttons are automatically labeled Command1, Command2, Command3, and so on. You can customize these controls using the Properties window. The easiest way to display the Properties window is to right click on an object and select Properties from the pop-up menu. Or, you can use the properties button located on the main toolbar.

The Properties window contains a property sheet that displays property names along the left side and settings along the right. To change the name of a command button, for example, you would select the button, display the Properties window, and then change the Caption property to something a bit more appropriate.

Forms

As was said earlier, a form is just another name for a window. You can customize each form using the Properties window just as you would any other control. Even though forms are the most superficial part of a working prototype, they are still the most important. All your efforts go into making these as attractive and intuitive as humanly possible. Think of each form as a blank canvas calling out, "I am your window of opportunity, so make me look good!"

Code Windows

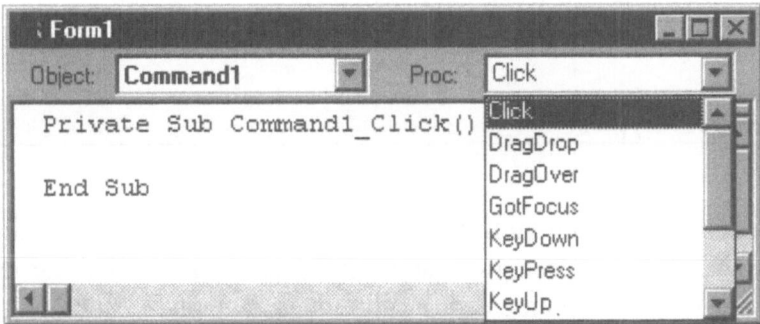

After you place controls on a form (using the Toolbox), and customize the way they look (with the Properties window), you are ready to begin writing code. The Code window is a behind the scenes look at a form. It reveals the list of events to which each object in your form can respond. Looking at the picture above, you can see that the command button named "Command1" is the current object and all its events are displayed on the right.

When writing code, you must first decide from what object you want to do something, and to what event you wish to respond. In the case of a command button, this is more often than not the Click event. For example, you may want to open another window when the user clicks on a button. Adding code to the button's Click event is the way you would do this.

One of the most important objects that appears in the Object drop-down list is the form itself. The Form object has one particular event that you'll want to pay close attention to as you design your prototype: that is the Load event. Whenever a form is first displayed, its Load event gets executed. From this event, you can initialize your form. For example, you may want to add items to a drop-down list. This way, when your form is displayed, it will look just like a window of a real product.

Types of Prototypes

In this section we examine the various kinds of prototypes you can employ. We take a close look at everything, from not having a prototype at all, to implementing a fully interactive one.

Now that we've looked at the Visual Basic integrated development environment, we can begin building a prototype. Well, that may not be entirely true. It largely depends on what kind of prototype you want to build and how much programming experience you have. Remember, this chapter is not meant to teach you how to program with Visual Basic, but rather, it is intended to show you what is involved in creating a prototype using a tool such as VB. Then, if you decide you want to use Visual Basic (which I'm sure you will), you can pick up a copy of it and, if need be, go through its online tutorial, "Learning Microsoft Visual Basic."

Prototype? What Prototype?

Who says you need to have a prototype? As a matter of fact, you don't. As long as you're the developer, the designer, and the owner of your company you can get away without having a prototype. As a matter of fact, you can get away with practically anything in that case, that is, except for fooling your customers. In all seriousness though, you really should have some kind of prototype. Even if it is at the very lowest level of the totem pole.

Simple Screen Shots

At the lowest level, you can create a cardboard cutout of each screen. Don't take that literally. By cardboard cutout I mean a picture that has no functionality at all. This kind of prototype provides no level of interactivity whatsoever. By using some of the design techniques discussed in Chapter Two, you can create static bitmaps of your screens. However, there is a drawback to using static bitmaps as a prototype. Even though you can iron out a lot of the aesthetic issues this way, you never really get a good sense of how well it is going to flow once it is implemented.

Another potential drawback with this type of prototype is the possibility that the designer has chosen to use bitmaps, instead of an interactive prototype, due to a lack of technical expertise. And, if you recall, that can be a bad thing in and of itself.

Navigational Prototypes

Simple screen shots cannot convey an idea nearly as well as a navigational prototype can. By navigational, I refer to a prototype that is designed to simulate only the navigational characteristics of a potential product. In other words, even though each screen does not do much of anything (because it is simply a collection of static bitmaps and/or dead controls), the user is still able to navigate around the product and see how screens relate to one another.

Using VB to Create a Navigational Prototype

Once you've designed a screen with a paint program, you are ready to place the bitmap into a Visual Basic form. The advantage to this kind of approach, over a noninteractive one, is that the bitmap (representing the content area of the window) is placed inside a real window. Instead of having a series of dead images that simply look like windows, your prototype can be comprised of actual windows. These windows can then appear when and where they're supposed to, just like the product-to-be.

A Visual Basic form can display a bitmap using three different techniques: via the form's Picture property, using a PictureBox control, or with an Image control.

Displaying a bitmap via a form's Picture property...

If the bitmap you want to place in your form consists of the entire content area of the window, then using a form's Picture property is the easiest route to take. To do this, simply select the form you want to use, open the Properties window, and click on the ellipsis button that appears to the right of the Picture property (shown above). This will open the common File Open dialog. From there, you can locate and choose a bitmap file. Or, alternatively, you can simply use the clipboard to paste an image into the form's Picture property.

Displaying a bitmap using a PictureBox control...

Another easy way to include a graphic in a form is by using the PictureBox control. You can add a PictureBox to a form using the same technique you would to add any other control: by double-clicking on its button in the Toolbox. The advantage to using a PictureBox control is that the bitmap can appear anywhere inside the window. It is not fastened to the top left-hand corner as it is when the Picture property of the form is used. Also, you can have as many of them as you want, and a PictureBox can contain other controls such as command buttons and option buttons. This makes moving a group of controls much easier.

Once you've placed a PictureBox on a form, the process of adding a bitmap to it is no different than it is for a form. You simply select the PictureBox, open the properties window, and change its Picture property.

Displaying a bitmap with an Image control...

Instead of using a PictureBox control, it is much more efficient to use the image control. It works identically to the PictureBox control with the exception that it cannot contain other controls. This lack of overhead makes the Image control much more memory-efficient.

Designating the startup form...

Once your forms look the way you want them to look, you're ready to link them together. This will allow your prototype to simulate the flow of the real product. First, however, you must decide what window is the primary window (you should already know that by this point) and designate it as the project's startup form. You can do this by selecting the Option command from the Tools menu and then clicking on the Project tab. This tells Visual Basic which form should be loaded first when the program is run.

Using controls to display forms...

Now you're ready for the big time! The moment you've been waiting for. How do you get this collection of well-designed forms to talk to one another? The answer is: by using controls. Obviously, you'll have to have thought out the navigation details in advance. For example, you'll probably want a menu bar that gives access to most of your forms or, perhaps, buttons that open other windows. You get the idea.

Adding a menu control to a form is easy; you simply use the Menu Editor command from the Tools menu. The Menu Editor allows you to add menus and menu items. Each menu object you create with the Menu Editor adds a new object to the current form's Code window, just as when you add a control.

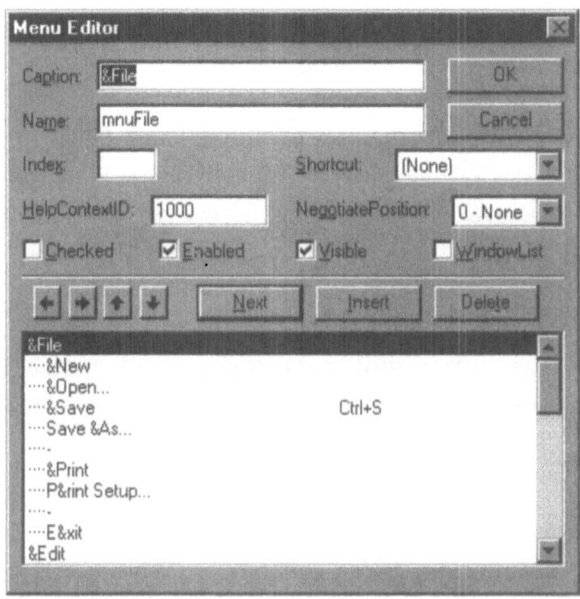

The Visual Basic Menu Editor window.

In addition to using a menu control, you can also use other controls to add navigation to your prototype. Command buttons, for example, are often used to open other windows. Also, if your screen bitmap has an area on it that you would like to allow the user to click on, you can place an image control over it. Then, using the Image control's Click event, you can make it do what it's supposed to do.

So how do you open one window from another? It's quite simple. First, you open the Code window for the form from which you want to start. Then, you choose the object from which the action is to take place. You select one of its events (usually the Click event). And, finally, you add the following line of code, "*formname*.Show." Where *formname* is the name of the form you want to open. Just as easily, you can also close an open form by writing "Unload *formname*." Not too bad, huh?

As you can see, learning the syntax of the Visual Basic programming language is definitely your biggest obstacle when it comes to creating navigational prototypes. However, by learning just a few simple commands, as you just saw, you'll be able to create them without any problem, regardless of how much (or how little) programming experience you've had. The ability to create navigational prototypes will make you a much better designer by allowing you to effectively communicate your product ideas.

Interactive Prototypes

The next step up from a navigational prototype is an interactive prototype. An interactive prototype is as close as you can get to the real thing. In addition to simply demonstrating the navigational aspects of a product, an interactive prototype also allows the user to try out its various features. Nothing can demonstrate the true look and feel of a product more than the ability to take it for a test drive.

Because an interactive prototype is primarily made up of smoke and mirrors, you need not worry about nearly as many technicalities as you would if you were creating a real application. For example, take a hypothetical inventory tracking system. Instead of using an actual database you can fake one. By adding data directly from your code, you can make it look as though it's coming from somewhere else. Or perhaps you're planning on incorporating a sophisticated online ordering feature as part of the inventory tracking system. To prototype it, you don't need to know the slightest thing about communications. Instead, you can simply simulate a modem connection.

Using VB to Create an Interactive Prototype

If you're planning on creating an interactive prototype with Visual Basic, you'll definitely need to take a look at the Programmer's Guide that comes with it, if you haven't already done so. Although you can get away with creating a navigational prototype by learning just a few basic commands and techniques, you'll need to know a whole lot more if you want your prototype to provide any significant level of interactivity. This doesn't mean, however, that you have to have a degree in computer science. Reading some of the Programmer's Guide should give you plenty enough know-how for creating an interactive prototype. If you want to create a real application, on the other hand, you'll need to read a little bit more.

Allowing a user to interact with a prototype in much the same way that she would interact with a real application requires, in many cases, almost just as much work. You never fully realize just how many little details need to be ironed out in a design until you've spent some time trying to get a prototype to behave the way the real product should. For example, should a particular control be disabled during a lengthy process or until a specific requirement has been met? If something changes on one window does something else need to be changed in another? Little issues such as these become extremely evident during the development of an interactive prototype. Of course, that's another benefit of creating an interactive prototype. It not only gives you a great way of presenting your ideas to others, it also gives you the chance to clarify some of the finer points of your design.

In this section, we take a look at how you can use Visual Basic to create an interactive prototype. In particular, we look at how creating an interactive prototype differs from creating a navigational one.

Using controls instead of bitmaps...

The biggest difference between an interactive prototype and a navigational prototype is the use of active controls instead of static bitmaps and/or inactive controls. Because each control works differently from the rest, you should become familiar with the properties, events, and methods of every control you plan to use. How you add and remove items from a list box, for instance, is entirely different from how you would add and remove items from a list view control.

Filling list-type controls with sample data...

An interactive prototype needs to look and feel just like the real thing. So, whether you're using list boxes, drop-down list boxes, combo boxes, list view controls, or tree view controls, you'll want to make sure that all your list-type controls are displayed with sample data. In addition, you may want to default your drop-down list boxes to a particular item.

Real-World Issue:
What's the best way to add sample data to a list box?

```
Place this code in a form's load event:

With MyList
        .AddItem "Item1"
        .AddItem "Item2"
        .AddItem "Item3"
        .AddItem "ItemN"
        .ListIndex = 0 ' Default to 1st item
End With
```

Faking feedback...

Remember, the key here is to make it look (and feel) real. So if something is suppose to take a long time, fake it! You'll want to make sure that you're using the system clock whenever you intentionally slow things down. This way, response time will always be the same, regardless of individual system performance.

Visual Basic provides you with a variety of ways to mimic actual response times. When it comes to slowing things down a bit, consider using the timer control. The timer control has an interval property that determines how often the timer control should do something. Also, there is a timer function that returns the number of seconds that have elapsed since midnight. You can use this to keep track of elapsed time.

In terms of faking visual feedback, you can change the mouse pointer to an hourglass, use progress bars, or just about anything else you want to do, such as faking a modem connection.

Logically responding to events...

As you can see, there is a lot more than meets the eye to making an interactive prototype. To do all these things, you'll need to become much more familiar with Visual Basic. Instead of just displaying one form from another, you'll need to logically respond to events and to develop an overall architecture for your prototype, however simple it may be. For instance, when the user clicks on a button, you not only want to display a form, but you also want to initialize the form by loading any sample data that it is going to display. How you choose to do this requires some forethought. Do you want to add the sample data directly from the form where the click event takes place? Or do you want to add the sample data from the form that is being loaded after the click event takes place? By making these kinds of decisions, you are, in a sense, defining an architecture for your prototype.

Finding a Balance

In the end, you'll probably find that the most effective and efficient method of prototyping is one that lies somewhere between a purely navigational and a fully interactive one. Why spend too much time prototyping a section that isn't as pivotal as another? When deciding on what kind of approach to take, ask yourself the following question, "What features will be the most frequently used?" These are the features for which you'll want to create an interactive prototype. This way, you'll be able to test them out ahead of time, and get out all their quirks. In other places, where functionality isn't nearly as important, using the navigational approach or a simple screen shot may be all that is necessary.

Beyond Prototyping

So what happens next? Once you've created a prototype you'll want to try it out on some users. And then, if need be, you'll have to redesign, prototype, and test all over again. This can go on and on until you're finally comfortable with your design, at which point you're ready to move on to the next phase: development. Depending on the type of organization you work at, handing your programmers a prototype may be all that is necessary. If things are more formal, you may need to create a specification document that explains the detailed flow and interface rules to which adherence is necessary.

Then again, you could always create a fully functional prototype with VB. If you did that, you'd be golden, because you'd have the final product in the palm of your hand.

Developing with VB

If Visual Basic is going to be used as the development platform, there are a couple of things that should be done differently during the prototype phase. These things will help save much time and effort down the road.

For starters, make sure that every control is given a descriptive and accurate name. Instead of settling for a control's default name (e.g., Command1, Text1, List1), assign each control a new name—using its Name property. Make sure that you follow the standard VB naming convention, which calls for a prefix to identify the type of control followed by a word or two that describes the control's purpose (e.g., cmdOK, txtUserName, lstCountry). As you can see, this will make your code much more legible. Not only will you be able to tell what type of control it is, but you'll also know what purpose it serves.

Naming conventions for VB...

Object/Data Type	Prefix	Example
Combo box	cbo	cboColor
Check box	chk	chkBackupFiles
Command button	cmd	cmdCancel
Form	frm	frmMain
Frame	fra	fraChoices
Image	img	imgLogo
Label	lbl	lblGeneral
List box	lst	lstCountries
MDI child form	mdi	mdiDocument

Menu	mnu	mnuFileOpen
Option button	opt	optSpeed
Panel (3d)	pnl	pnlStatus
Picture box	pic	picBackground
Text box	txt	txtName
Timer	tmr	tmrAnimate
Array	a	aUsers
Boolean	b	bDirty
Currency	c	cAmount
Double	d	dGravity
Date	dt	dtBegin
Integer	i	iCounter
Single	f	fPercent
String	s	sTemp
Variant	v	vData

Secondly, do not embed code in strange and weird places. By that I mean, take the time to develop a consistent architecture. For example, if you're initializing data in more than one place, consider creating an Initialize subroutine where all of your initialization code can reside.

In the end, there is no substitute for a solid programming background. Being able to create a prototype with VB does not necessarily mean that you'll be able to carry out the next crucial step of bringing a product into fruition. So, like with everything else, read, practice, read, and practice. Only then will you succeed.

Epilogue

If you take only one thing with you after reading this book, let it be simplicity. This will, in and of itself, make you a better interface designer. Always remember: It is far easier to design something that is complicated than it is to design something that is simple.

One thing we haven't discussed enough–considering aesthetics is such an integral part of interface design–is the idea that beauty is in the eyes of the beholder. As you design your software, remember, everybody has different tastes, some good and some bad; some will like your ideas, some will hate them. When it comes to look and feel, you'll never be able to please everyone. By keeping things simple, though, you'll be sure to reduce the number of unhappy users. As long as you stick to the guidelines discussed in this book, you can rest assured that you've done your best. So don't let other people's negative viewpoints bring you down. Instead, learn from them, whenever possible.

As time goes on, you'll begin to develop your own sense of style. Creativity is a fire that burns inside all of us. The more wood you throw on it, the hotter the fire burns. The guidelines and ideas discussed in this book are only intended to help keep you on the right track. It's important that you cultivate your own ideas. No one wants a bunch of applications that look and feel identical to each other. What we want are applications that behave the way we've come to expect them to behave. This way, we don't have to kee-plearning how to use them over and over again. Once something has been perfected, and has come to be widely accepted, what right do we have to mess with it? This is what guidelines are all about. On the other hand, if you have a better way of doing something, go for it. Keep the wheels of ingenuity turning. This is how guidelines are established.

When it comes to interface design, everybody thinks he's a Picasso! Learning to work in an environment where your own sense of design must sometimes be compromised with others' is of utmost importance. Unless you're self-employed, chances are that the product you're working on is not yours to claim. By that I mean, don't take things so seriously that you begin to think you're always right and no one else has the right to be heard. Your goal should be to design the best possible product, and that means learning to realize when someone else has a better way of doing something. Watch out for pride; it has a way of keeping you from getting what you really want.

As you continue on your journey, take some time to think about the future of interface design. Is interface design an art with an end? In other words, here we are doing everything we possibly can to make an application look like a masterpiece, when, in the end, it will only be around for a couple of years, at best. Should the lack of permanence change the way we approach interface design?

Or is it true, as they say, that anything worth doing is worth doing well? Who knows? Maybe interface design is one of the things by which future generations will judge the Information Age. Perhaps, somewhere in an art history class, sometime in the year 2609 our ancestors will be studying our work.

Regardless of what happens, I think interface design is a lot like painting. This is the reason why it is so difficult for an organization to create a great product. When was the last time you saw a great painting that was created by more than one artist?

Glossary

.3 extension The suffix, or extension, that is included as part of every filename. It can be up to three characters long and is always preceded by a period. The extension helps both the system and the user identify what type of file it is.

32-bit Bigger, faster, and better than 16-bits.

A

about box A dialog box that identifies a product's version number and/or legal copyright. It is opened by selecting the "About..." command from the Help menu.

access key A keystroke that allows the user to activate a control without using the mouse. Every control that has a caption, such as buttons and menu items, can also have an access key, which is designated by an underlined character in the caption. Pressing the Ctrl key and access key simultaneously is the same as clicking on the object with the mouse.

alias *See* shortcut.

anti-aliasing A design technique that reduces the jagged appearance of curved and diagonal lines by blurring adjacent pixels using average colors.

B

bitmap An image that is comprised of rows and columns of pixels.

blend A design technique that is used to fade one color into another.

Boolean A logical system that represents two mutually exclusive conditions (i.e., Yes/No, On/Off, True/False, 0/1).

Briefcase A special type of folder in Windows 95 that helps synchronize files on two different computers.

button *See* command button.

C

cancel button The command button that closes a dialog box or message box without causing any action to be performed. The cancel button is automatically clicked when the ESCape key is pressed. There can only be one cancel button on a window.

caption The textual portion of a control, which identifies its function or purpose.

cascading menu A submenu that is displayed when a menu item is selected. Cascading menus allow menus to be organized hierarchically.

character-based An interface that is nongraphical and only able to display ASCII characters.

check box A two-state button that represents on/off, yes/no, or true/false. Check boxes can also provide a third state, for handling situations such as all/some/none.

child window A window whose movement and display is restricted to within the boundaries of another window (which is often called the parent, or MDI, window).

click 1. The act of pressing the left mouse button while the mouse pointer is over a clickable object. 2. An onomatopoeic representation of the sound that is made when a mouse button is pressed.

clipboard A temporary location for storing data that has been cut or copied using the Edit menu. This data can be moved or replicated via the paste command.

close The process of shutting down a window.

collection A group of related objects. For example, a collection called Cars can be comprised of Audis, BMWs, and Chevrolets.

combo box A combination of an edit box and a list box. This allows the user to either select from a list of choices or enter a different response altogether. *See also* drop-down combo box.

command button A control that has a definitive visual border and represents an action. A single mouse click initiates the action.

common dialogs A set of prefabricated dialogs that are provided by Windows in order to ensure that applications have the same look and feel during common operations such as opening a file or setting up a printer.

container 1. A object that is comprised of other objects that may not necessarily be related. A car, for example, can be considered a container for seat objects. 2. An application that is capable of linking or embedding objects provided by another application (OLE server).

context-sensitive Something that is related to the presence of an existing object or condition.

control An object that allows the user to take action.

Control Panel A collection of icons that allow the user to specify custom settings and alter the way in which hardware devices and system software operate within the Windows environment.

cursor *See* mouse pointer.

custom control Any control that is not part of the standard Windows control set.

D

data-centric A design model in which the data is the core of the product. A data-centric application appears more like data that can be manipulated than like an application that manipulates data.

default button The button that is automatically clicked when the Enter key is pressed. There can only be one default button on a window.

desktop The place on the computer from which all work is done. The Windows 95 shell metaphor is based on a hierarchy of objects, and the desktop metaphor is at the top of this hierarchy.

dialog box A modal window that allows communication, or an exchange of information, to take place between the user and the software.

directory *See* folder.

dithering A design technique that allows a bitmap containing a limited set of colors to appear as though there are many more colors. By alternating one color with another, a new color is created.

DLL *See* dynamic-link library.

document A file that is created and supported by a data-centric application.

double-click The act of rapidly pressing the left mouse button twice while the mouse pointer is over a clickable object.

drag and drop The action of selecting an object and, while holding down the mouse button, moving it over a target object before releasing the mouse button.

drop-down combo box A combination of an edit box and a drop-down list box. This allows the user to either select from a list of choices or enter a different response altogether. *See also* combo box.

drop-down list box A control that allows the user to select an item from a list of choices. The list portion of the control can be shown or hidden.

drop-down menu The menu that is displayed when a menu bar title is clicked.

drop shadow A design technique that gives a two-dimensional object the appearance that it is floating above the background.

dynamic link library (DLL) A file that contains precompiled code that can be used by other running applications.

E

edit box A standard control that allows the user to type in a response ranging anywhere from one character to a multi-line memo. Otherwise known as a text box.

Edit menu A common drop-down menu that is used for commands that affect the current object, such as Cut, Copy, and Paste.

embedding The ability of an OLE container application to insert and save, in its own document, an object that was created by another OLE savvy application.

event Any action that can be responded to by an application.

event-driven programming A style of programming in which the flow of code is determined by the various events that take place in the system.

Explorer The Windows 95 file manager, which not only maintains folders and files, but can also be used to navigate the entire system.

extended selection A method of selecting and deselecting more than one item in a multi-select list box. Extended selection allows the current selection to be extended, or shrunk, in either a contiguous (using the Shift key) or disjoint manner (using the Ctrl key). *See also* simple selection.

F

File menu A common drop-down menu that is used for all document-related commands, such as New, Open, Save, Save As, and Print.

focus A control is said to "have focus" once the user has selected it and has made it the active control. This is typically done by using the tab key, or with the mouse.

folder A metaphor for a file directory. Folders can contain a collection of files as well as other folders.

font A graphical character set that is based on a particular typeface and style.

form *See* window.

frame *See* window frame.

G

group box A container control that allows you to group related controls together, providing your interface with a higher level of clarity.

H

handle A point on a frame that allows you to resize an object using a mouse.

help authoring system An online help development environment that keeps you from having to understand the intricacies of rich-text format files.

help contents file A file (.cnt) that contains a hierarchical list of items that will be displayed in the Help Topics window.

help file A help project file (.hpj), or an individual rich-text format file (.rtf), that has been compiled into a help file (.hlp) using the Windows help compiler. The help file can then be opened using the WinHelp application.

Help menu A common drop-down menu that is used to access the Help Topics window and about box.

help project file A text file (.hpj) that describes to the help compiler the list of files, topics, and settings that should be used to create the help file.

Help Topics window A tabbed dialog that displays an application's online help table of contents, index, and find page.

hotspot graphic A graphic that appears in a help file and has multiple clickable regions.

icon A special type of bitmap that typically measures only 16 x 16, 32 x 32, or 48 x 48 pixels. An icon differs from a bitmap because it has the ability to include transparent and/or inverted pixels and can be associated with a file.

in-place activation The ability to edit another application's embedded or linked data directly from a container application.

integrated design utility The portion of an integrated development environment that allows the developer to design an interface by placing controls and setting their properties.

integrated development environment (IDE) A software development tool that includes an integrated design utility, a code editor, a compiler, and a debugger all in one.

interactive prototype A prototype that allows users to interact with it in much the same way they could with a real product.

jaggies The appearance of unevenness that can occur when drawing a curved or diagonal line using pixels that are discernible to the naked eye.

jump text Any word that brings the user to a different topic when it is clicked with the mouse. Jump text appears in help files and is usually green and underlined with a single or dotted line.

L

label A static text control that identifies another control or conveys information to the user.

light source An imaginary light that determines the way three-dimensional objects should be shaded. The Windows common light source emanates from the top left of the screen and shines diagonally down to the bottom right corner.

linking The ability of an OLE container application to insert a file, or part of a file, that was created by another OLE savvy application into its own document.

list box A control that displays a list of items in a scrolling window. *See also* multi-select list box and single-select list box.

list view A list control that allows the user to view items using one of four ways: large icons, small icons, list, and details.

logo program The guidelines and procedures that allow an application to legally use the "Designed for Microsoft Windows 95" logo.

M

Macintosh Now is as good a time as any to pay homage to the Macintosh. I haven't mentioned it once in this book and by no means do I intend not to give it the credit it deserves. We all owe our deepest thanks to what it has done to the face of software. Three cheers for the Mac!

macro A command or series of commands that allow you to customize the basic functionality of a system.

main help window The type of window that is used to display reference help. A main help window has both a menu bar and a button bar.

maximize To expand a window to its largest possible size.

MDI *See* multiple document interface.

menu A vertical list of items from which the user can make a choice. *See also* pull-down menu and pop-up menu.

menu bar The horizontal list of menu titles that appears directly below a window's title bar.

menu button A button that displays a pop-up menu when clicked.

menu item An individual choice that appears on a menu.

menu negotiation The way in which it is decided how a container application should combine its menu titles together with those of another application during OLE in-place activation.

menu title An individual choice that appears on a menu bar.

message box A modal dialog that is used to convey information, ask a question, or alert the user.

method A way to do something with an object. For example, a list box control has an AddItem and a RemoveItem method.

minimize To shrink a window down to its smallest size, a window button.

mnemonic *See* access key.

modal A situation in which the user is temporarily restricted from an action that would otherwise be readily available.

modeless Any situation in which the user is not being restricted from activating other windows.

mouse Any of various small rodents having a pointed snout, small ears, elongated body, and slender tail.

mouse pointer A graphical cursor that moves in direct relation with a mouse.

multi-select list box A list box that allows the user to select one or more items, much as a list of check boxes would. *See also* extended selection and simple selection.

multiple document interface (MDI) A document-based design model that uses a parent window and one or more child windows, each of which can have a different document open at any given time.

multiple resolution bitmap A bitmap that has been compiled with the Multi-Resolution Bitmap Compiler (Mrbc.exe). This enables you to create bitmaps that compensate for differences between aspect ratios and resolutions.

N

navigational prototype A prototype that allows the user to navigate and see the various proposed screens and how they relate to one another.

Network Neighborhood A Windows 95 icon that represents networked connections and devices.

○

object Something that is identifiable to the user as an entity in and of itself. Jargon for a noun, if you will.

object-oriented An organization model that relies heavily on the distinction between nouns and verbs.

object linking and embedding (OLE) The technology that allows an application to use another application's objects and/or services. *See also* embedding and linking.

option button A type of button that is used in groups of two or more and presents a set of mutually exclusive choices to the user. When one option button is on, all others in the same group are off.

P

palette *See* tool window.

pane A logical portion of a window that can be used to contain controls.

parent window An MDI window that is capable of containing one or more child windows. *See also* multiple-document interface.

picture button A command button that has an icon and, possibly, an optional caption.

pixel The smallest addressable element of the screen.

pop-up menu A menu that is displayed in a way other than via a menu bar.

pop-up menu button A two state button that displays a pop-up menu when depressed.

primary window The main window of an application.

progress bar A control that is used to provide the user with live feedback indicating the current state of a process.

properties The characteristics that define an individual object.

prototype A model that is used to represent the possible design of a potential product.

pull-down menu A menu that is displayed via a menu bar.

R

radio button *See* option button.

Recycle Bin A Windows 95 icon that displays the collection of every hard drive's Recycled directory.

reference help Documentation style help text that is displayed in a main help window.

Registry A global repository for all application-specific configuration settings. The registry itself is a file (REG.DAT) that is organized into a hierarchical list.

resolution   The number of horizontal and vertical pixels that make up the screen (i.e., 640 x 480, 800 x 600, or 1024 x 768).

resource editor   A software development utility that is used to create dialogs, icons, and bitmaps.

restore   To resize a window back to its previous dimensions as it was prior to a maximize or minimize event.

rich text box   An enhanced edit box control that is capable of supporting multiple fonts, text attributes, and complex formatting.

rich-text format   A special type of text file that is able to store, along with the text, complex formatting information.

right-click   The act of pressing the right mouse button while the mouse pointer is over a clickable object. This typically displays a context-sensitive pop-up menu.

S

screen shot   A bitmap that represents a copy of an individual window or of the entire screen. This is done by pressing Alt-Print Screen or Print Screen, respectively.

scroll bar   An interface control that is used to pan up and down or from left and right. This allows what would otherwise be hidden to be viewed using a limited amount of screen space.

SDI   *See* single document interface.

secondary window   Any application window, or dialog, other than the primary window.

select To choose one item among many.

server An application that is able to provide services or objects to other applications.

Shaker A style of design that emphasizes simplicity and function above all else.

shortcut 1. A file that points to another file or object. 2. A keyboard equivalent or access key. 3. A type of button that is used in task help to automate tasks.

simple selection A method of selecting and deselecting more than one item in a multi-select list box. Clicking on an item once selects it; clicking on it again deselects it. *See also* extended selection.

single document interface (SDI) An application design model that is capable of displaying only one document at a time using a primary window. There are no child windows in an SDI application.

single-select list box A list box that allows the user to select only one item, much as a list of option buttons would.

size grip A handle that has a permanent visual presence and helps you resize a window. The size grip usually appears at the bottom rightmost corner of a resizable window.

slider A graphical control that can be used to specify values within a fixed range.

spin box A piggyback control that works in conjunction with an edit box and is used to increment or decrement numerical values.

splash screen An initial window that welcomes the user and identifies the product.

split bar A line shaped control that divides two panes and allows the size of one to be increased while the other is decreased.

status bar A control that resides along the bottom edge of a primary window and is used to provide informative text for the user.

status notification item An item that resides on the taskbar and allows the user to monitor and, in some cases, modify the current state of the system (e.g., remaining memory, volume settings, video resolution, or incoming mail).

sticky button A picture button that behaves like a check box or an option button.

tab focus *See* focus.

tab strip A type of control that uses a folder tab metaphor to contain, and help organize, controls that would otherwise require more space and/or multiple dialogs.

taskbar The area of the Windows 95 desktop that displays the Start menu, window buttons, and status notification items.

task help Procedure-oriented help text that is displayed in a step-by-step format using a task help window.

text box *See* edit box.

ticker text A label that is used to display progress information.

title bar The top part of a window that is used to display a title and to control its current state.

toolbar A control that provides button access to an application's commonly used features.

toolbar button *See* picture button.

toolbar negotiation The way in which it is decided how a container application should display its toolbars together with those of another application during OLE in-place activation.

tool tip A pop-up label control that displays context-sensitive help.

tool window A type of secondary window that is used to display a group of different tools or choices.

topic An addressable page of a help file.

tree view A control that allows the user to view a hierarchical list of items.

U

UI bulking A design technique that gives the illusion of a bigger and better product by emphasizing that which is visible.

UNC pathname A file-naming convention that allows net-worked resources to be accessed without the use of drive letters.

V

View menu A common drop-down menu that contains items relating to the way in which data is displayed.

W

window *See* primary window and secondary window.

window button A minimized window.

window frame The outermost edge, or border, of a window. The type of frame determines if, and in what way, a window can be resized.

window manipulation buttons *See* close, maximize, minimize, and restore.

Window menu A common drop-down menu used to maintain a list of open child windows within an MDI application.

wizard A type of user assistance in which a continuous set of related dialogs are used in order to simplify what would other-wise be a complex task.

Index

.3 extension, 159
32-bit, 159

About box, 30, 159
Access key, 159
Add/Remove Programs feature, 80
Aesthetic appeal, xvi
Aesthetics, 10, 155
Alias, 71
Animated icons, 38
Anti-aliasing, 11, 159
Appeal, aesthetic, xvi
Application Programming Interface,
  131-132
Application-specific menus, 55
Applications
  document-based, 47
  marketable, 28-32
ASCII character set, 2

Back button, 118-119
Barker, Bart, xiii-xiv
Battery, warning for, 88
Beauty, 39
Bitmaps, 21, 26, 127, 160
  256-color, 26
Blends, 13, 160
Boolean condition, 59, 160
Boxes
  check, 58-59
  combo, 60
  dialog, 44, 49-50
  edit, 59-60
  group, 65

list, 61-64
message, 50-51
rich text, 60
spin, 60
Briefcase, 79-80, 160
Button bar, 106, 111
Buttons, 56-59
  browse, 111
  cancel, 57, 118, 160
  command, 56-57
  default, 57
  menu, 58
  option, 59
  picture, 57-58
  sticky, 57

Calvo, Alex, xiii
Cancel button, 57, 118, 160
Caption, 160
Cascading menu, 160
Character-based systems, 2, 160
Check boxes, 58-59, 161
Child windows, 48, 161
Click, 161
Clipboard, 161
  Windows, 23, 27
Close, 161
Code window of Visual Basic, 1
  41-142
Collections of objects, 42, 161
Color
  inverted, 21
  pixel, 12
  transparent, 21

Combo boxes, 60, 161
COMCTL32.DLL dynamic-link
    library, 84
Command buttons, 56-57, 161
Common dialog, 161
Common light source, 13-14
Comparing files, 82
Compatibility
  32-bit, 86
  Windows 95 software, 86-89
  Windows NT, 87
Compound objects, 7-8
Compressing files, 82
Consistency, 9-10, 36-37
Container, 162
Contents file, 121, 128-129
Contents page of Help Topics
    window,   100
Context-sensitive help, 92-98, 162
Control Panel, 79, 162
Controls, 52-70, 162
  types of, 52-67
CPL files, 79
Creativity, 155
Cursors, hourglass, 38
Custom controls, 25, 162
Customizable workspace, 71

Data-centricity, 40-42, 162
Default buttons, 57, 162
Design
  object-oriented, 7-8, 40-41
  side-by-side, 20-21
Design concepts, 6, 35-42
Design principles, xv
Design time, 134-135
Design utilities, integrated, 24-25
"Designed for Microsoft Windows
    95" logo, 85

Designing
  menus, 56
  for users, 35-40
Desktop, 71, 72, 163
Dialog
  common, 161
  modal, 51
Dialog boxes, 44, 49-50, 163
Dithering, 12-13, 163
Document, 163
Document-based applications, 47
"Document Name-Application
    Name" naming convention, 87
Document windows, 47
DOS, 2
Double-click, 163
Drag and drop, 163
Drop-down combo box, 163
Drop-down list box, 62, 164
Drop-down menus, 30, 44, 164
Drop-shadow, 14, 164
Dynamic link library (DLL), 79,
    164

Edit boxes, 59-60, 164
Edit menu, 54-55, 164
Ellipses, 50, 57
Embedding objects, 69, 164
Enter key, 57
Escape key, 57
Event, 164
Event-driven programming,
    135-136, 164
Exclamation type message box, 51
Explorer, 165
Extended selection, 165

F1 key, 97-98
Feedback, visual, 37-38

File folders, 36
File Manager, 77
File menu, 53-54, 165
  standard, 47
File names, long, 87
Files
  comparing, 82
  compressing, 82
Find page of Help Topics window,
  103-104
Finish button, 118
Floating toolbars, 49
Focus, 165
Folder, 165
Font, 165
Footnotes, 122-123
Forgiving interface design, 37
Frames of windows, 43

Graphical user interface (GUI),
  xi-xiii
  advent of, 2
  designing, xi, *see also* Interface
  design
  help with, *see* Online help for
  application user
  words with, 16-17
Graphics, 113
Group boxes, 65, 166
GUI, *see* Graphical user interface
Guidelines, Windows interface,
  see Windows interface
  guidelines

Handles of windows, 43, 166
Help authoring systems, 130, 166
Help button, 98
Help contents file, 166
Help file, 166

Help menu, 55, 166
Help project file, 121, 126-127,
  166
Help Topics window, 99-104, 166
Hierarchical topics list, 99-102
Hierarchy of objects in
  Windows 95 shell, 75
Hotspot graphics, 113, 167
Hourglass cursors, 38

Icon editor, 21
Icon museum, 21-22
Icons, 10, 73-74, 167
  animated, 38
Image control, 145-146
In-place activation, 69-70, 167
Index page of Help Topics
  window, 101-102
Initialization files (INI files), 82
Insert Object dialog box, 68
Installation, 80-82
Installation log file, 81-82
Installation software, 81-82
Integrated design utilities, 24-25,
  167
Integrated development
  environment   (IDE), 167
Interactive canvas, interface design
  as, 19-32
Interactive prototypes, 148-152,
  167
Interface design, xv
  forgiving, 37
  future of, 156-157
  as interactive canvas, 19-32
  techniques, 19-23
  testing, 39-40
  tools for, 24-27

Interface guidelines, Windows, *see*
  Windows interface guidelines
Inverted color, 21

Jaggies, 11, 167
Jump text, 107, 167
Jumps, 112, 124

Label, 168
Label control, 64-65
Layout comparison, 22-23
Light source, 168
Lighting, 13-14
Linking objects, 68, 168
List boxes, 61-64, 168
List-type controls, 150
List view control, 62-63, 78, 168
Logo program, 168
Long file names, 87

Macintosh, 168
Macros, 124-125, 169
Mail-enabled File menu, 89
Main toolbar window of Visual
  Basic, 137
Main help windows, 109-113, 169
Managing Your Money 10, 4
Marketable applications, 28-32
Maximize, 169
MDI (multiple document interface),
  47-49
Menu bar, 44, 110, 169
Menu buttons, 58, 169
Menu Editor, 146-148
Menu items, 44, 169
  types of, 53
Menu negotiation, 169
Menu title, 44, 169

Menus, 35, 52-56, 169
  designing, 56
  toolbars and, 70
Message box title bar text, 51
Message boxes, 50-51, 169
Messaging API (MAPI) Software
  Development Kit (SDK), 89
Methods, 41-42, 169
Microsoft, 1
Microsoft Help Workshop,
  126-129
Microsoft Money 95, 5
Microsoft Paint tool window, 49
Microsoft Visual Basic, *see* Visual
  Basic
Microsoft Windows NT, *see*
  Windows NT
Minimize, 170
Modal dialog, 51, 170
Modeless, 170
Modes, 35-36
Mouse, 170
Mouse pointer, 170
Multi-select list box, 61, 170
Multiple document interface (MDI),
  47-49, 170
Multiple resolution bitmaps, 113,
  170
Multistate check box, 58-59
My Computer icon and window,
  76-77

Navigational prototypes, 144-148,
  171
Network Neighborhood, 78, 171
Networking, peer-to-peer, 78
Next button, 118-119
Nonscrolling regions, 112,
  123-124

Object linking and embedding
  (OLE), 67, 171
 custom controls (OCX), 25
 objects in, 67
 support, 88-89
Object-oriented design, 7-8, 40-41,
  171
Objects, 7, 171
 collections of, 42
 compound, 7-8
 embedding, 69
 hierarchy of, in Windows 95
  shell, 75
 linking, 68
 in object linking and embedding
  (OLE), 67
 properties of, 41
 relationships between, 42
OLE, see Object linking and
  embedding
Online help for application user,
  91-132
 connecting, 131-132
 context-sensitive, 92-98
 creating, 120-130
 designing, 92-119
 F1 key, 97-98
 Help button, 98
 Help Topics window, 99-104
 reference help, 108-114
 task help, 104-107
 text in window, 92-93
 "What's This?" help, 94-97
 wizards, 115-119
Option buttons, 59, 171

Paint program, 23, 26
Pane, 171
Parent windows, 48, 172

Paste Special dialog box, 69
Peer-to-peer networking, 78
Picture buttons, 57-58, 172
PictureBox control, 145
Pixel, 172
Pixel color, 12
Plug and Play, 88
Pop-up menu button, 172
Pop-up menus, 52, 172
Portable Executable (PE) format,
  86
Primary windows, 47, 172
Problem, understanding, 6-7
Product-specific menus, 55
Progress indicators, 38, 65, 172
Project window of Visual Basic,
  138
Properties, 41, 134, 172
Properties window of Visual Basic,
  140-141
Prototypes, 172
 interactive, 148-152
 navigational, 144-148
 types of, 142-152
Prototyping, 40
Pull-down menus, 30, 44, 172

Quicken 3.0, 5

Recycle Bin, 78-79, 172
Reference counts, 87
Reference help, 108-114, 173
Registry Editor, 83
Registry for Windows 95 shell,
  82-83, 173
Related Topics button, 107
Relationships between objects, 42
Report view, 63
Resizable windows, 43, 44, 48

Resolution, 173
Resource editor, 24, 172
Restore, 173
Rich text boxes, 60, 173
Rich-text format files, 120-125,
    173
Right-click, 173
Run command, 80
Run time, 134

Screen, splash, 28-30
Screen design utilities, 25
Screen shots, 143, 173
Scroll bars, 45-46, 173
SDI (single document interface),
    47-49
Secondary help windows, 113-114
Secondary windows, 47, 173
Select, 174
Send Mail command, 89
Server, 174
Shaker, 174
Share-level access, 78
Shortcut, 71, 174
Shortcut buttons, 106-107
Shrink-wrapped design, 1
Side-by-side design, 20-21
Simple selection, 174
Simplicity, 15, 39, 155
Single document interface (SDI),
    47-49, 174
Single-select list box, 61, 174
Size grip, 43, 174
Slider control, 65-66, 174
Sloppiness, 37
Software, installation, 81-82
Software compatibility, Windows
    95, 86-89
Spin box, 175

Splash screen, 28-30, 174
Split bars, 46, 174
Spin boxes, 60
Standards, following, 8-9
Start button, 72
Startup time, 28
Status bars, 31, 38, 46, 93-94, 174
Status notification item, 175
Status notification utilities, 73
Sticky buttons, 57, 175

Tab strip, 66, 176
Task help, 104-107, 176
Taskbars, 72-73, 176
Tasks, 7
Testing, usability, 40
Text fields, 59-60
Thunking, 86
Ticker text, 38, 176
Title bars of windows, 43-44, 176
Tool tip control, 66
Tool tips, 30, 57-58, 93-94, 176
Tool windows, 49, 177
Toolbar negotiation, 176
Toolbars, 30-31, 44-45, 176
    floating, 49
    menus and, 70
Toolbox of Visual Basic, 139
Topic, 177
Topics Found dialog, 101-102
Topics list, hierarchical, 99-102
Transparent color, 21
Tree view control, 64, 77-78, 177

Ugliness, 39
UI bulking, 31-32, 177
Uninstaller, 81, 83

Universal Naming Convention (UNC), support, 89, 177
Usability testing, 40
User-friendliness, 18
User-level access, 78
Users, designing for, 35-40
Utilities
  integrated design, 24-25
  status notification, 73

VeriTest, 85
View menu, 55, 63, 177
Visual Basic, 25, 132-142
  custom controls (VBX), 25
  developing with, 153-154
Visual development tools, xv-xvi
Visual feedback, 37-38

Warning for battery, 88
"What's This?" help, 94-97
Window button, 177
Window manipulation buttons, 44, 178
Window menu, 55, 178
Windows, 42-51
  child, 48
  details of, 42-46
  document, 47
  handles of, 43
  parent, 48
  primary, 47
  resizable, 43, 44, 48
  secondary, 47
  title bars of, 43-44

types of, 47-51
Windows 3.1 splash screen, 29
Windows 95 common file Open dialog, 50
Windows 95 Control Panel, 74
Windows 95 environment, 71-83
Windows 95 Explorer window, 42
Windows 95 help system, *see* Online help for application user
Windows 95 logo program, 85
Windows 95 shell, 32, 74-80
  hierarchy of objects in, 75
  registry for, 82-83
  windows in, 76-80
Windows 95 software compatibility, 86-89
Windows 95 Start menu, 74
Windows API (Application Programming Interface), 131-132
Windows Explorer window, 77
Windows frame, 43, 177
Windows help browser, 121
Windows interface guidelines, 33-89
Windows Interface Guidelines for Software Design, 34
Windows NT 3.51, 84
Windows NT compatibility, 87
WISE Installer, 82
Wizard buttons, 118-119
Wizard windows, 117-119
Wizards, 115-119, 178
Workspace, customizable, 71

About the Author

Alex Calvo is 28 years old and was born in Buenos Aires, Argentina. He has always enjoyed design. Therefore when he graduated from Sacred Heart University in 1989 with a BS in Computer Science he found that mere programming was not going to be enough to satisfy his artistic appetite.

One day, while working on MECA Software's *Andrew Tobias' Managing Your Money*, something clicked, and it wasn't just the mouse! He realized that he had combined his technical background together with his sense of design in a harmonious way. From that moment on he became a human interface designer and consultant. After working on the design of *Managing Your Money for Windows 1.0* he left MECA to start his own company, fyi Software. *Managing Your Money* has since been touted as being "a breakthrough in ease-of-use" by magazines such as *PC/Computing*.

Using his programming expertise and Microsoft's Visual Basic, he created *The Carbuyers' Companion* and *The Homebuyers' Companion*, both of which were licensed to Parsons Technology (an Intuit company). Both products were called "two of the most attractive programs" by Walt Mossberg of *The Wall Street Journal*. Since that time he has developed four other programs (*College Search*, *B-School Search*, *Law School Search*, and *Med School Search*), all of which were sold to Kaplan InterActive. Alex has also been featured in the "Basic Heroes" column of the *Visual Basic Programmer's Journal* and is a certified Visual Basic developer.

The Craft of Windows 95 Interface Design is Alex's first book. He can be reached via email at 72154.2240@compuserve.com.